HUNTING SARACENS
AND MODERNISTS

HUNTING SARACENS
AND MODERNISTS:

Saving America and The West

by

DAVID G. BOLGIANO

HUNTING SARACENS
AND MODERNISTS

World Ahead Press is a division of WND Books. The views and opinions expressed in this book are those of the author and do not necessarily reflect the official policy or position or WND Books.

Paperback ISBN: 978-1-944212-62-9
eBook ISBN: 978-1-944212-63-6

Printed in the United States of America
16 17 18 19 20 21 LSI 9 8 7 6 5 4 3 2 1

CONTENTS

PREFACE

I n his beautifully written book, *The Great Heresies*, Roman Catholic apologist Hilaire Belloc identified five major moral threats to Christendom: Arianism, Mohammedanism, Albigensianism, Protestantism and what Belloc labeled the "Modern Attack." Arianism and Albigensianism were disputes of the early church concerning respectively the full Divinity of Christ and the duality of good and evil in the Universe. These disputes were mostly resolved in the first millennium AD The violent upheavals between Catholics and Protestants were a problem primarily confined to Europe and most of the bloody disputes between them were resolved after the Peace of Westphalia that capped the Thirty Years' War. The intellectual and spiritual rift between Roman Catholicism and Protestantism is still ongoing, yet it is a dispute that often fills pages with beautiful prose like that of John Henry Cardinal Newman, G. K. Chesterton, and other brilliant theologians on both sides of that rift.

As a Roman Catholic, I pray for this split to be mended, with all Christian churches coming together again under the guidance of Peter's successor. But, whether that happens in my lifetime is not an existential threat to The West. Nor are the existence of practicing Jews, Hindus and Buddhists. That leaves Mohammedanism and Modernity as the unresolved and ever-festering dangers to the good *(godly)* order and moral freedoms of the West's Judeo-Christian heritage so beautifully exemplified in the Declaration of Independence and our republic's other founding documents.

Also, adherents to Christianity, Judaism and most of the world's religions except Islam do not have violence as one of their core articles of faith. As Brian Hennessey of *Israel Today* recently argued, "extremism" isn't really the problem. It's which specific religion believers are following. "[T]he more serious a moderate Muslim gets about practicing his religion, the more 'radicalized' he will become," he contended. "With those that look to the Bible, just the opposite happens. The core message of the Bible urges believers to love your neighbors as yourself, not cut their heads off. So the more a Christian or Jew gets serious about his biblical beliefs, and practices them, the more loving and godly they become."[1]

With its Judeo-Christian roots, a truly free and classically liberal[2] society, which respects private property rights and allows men to freely follow God's grace that is deep in every person's heart, is the least imperfect of manmade societies. It is the society envisioned by our founding fathers as so clearly set forth in the *Federalist Papers*, Declaration of Independence, and our Constitution. The twin pillars of Islam and Modernity now perilously threaten it. By Modernity I mean that self-centric, condescending worldview of most Progressives, which foolishly believes that mankind can reach paradise here on Earth via advances in science, knowledge and sheer political will. It is, distilled down to its essence, original sin: elevating man to the status of God. It is most clearly seen in such excesses as transgenderism, whereby a male rebels against the genetic code God gave him, decides to become his own god by cutting off his penis and calling himself by a girl's name. Then, not satisfied with his own self-mutilation, demands that the rest of society join in his folly.

In an attack on all that is good and wholesome in America, the Progressive political machine affirms such insane acts and tries to coerce believers in the traditions of Christianity or Judaism to deny their one true God. It is happening as I write, federal and state prosecutors are drafting criminal charges against good and faithful people for simply living by God's Ten Commandments. Some believers are deluded from within their own churches by weak-willed pastors who, not wanting to offend anyone, follow a watered-down faith that has no roots in Scripture or grace. Most churches in the West have become people-centric versus God-centric in their themes, styles, and focus of worship. In my own church, the priest offering the sacrifice of Mass used to face God on the altar: Vatican II, like so many atrocities of the Sixties, turned the priest around, changed the lingua franca of Latin and made going to once sacred Mass more akin to a folk concert. The priest, rather than being in the image and order of Melchizedek, often became a Bob Dylan in vestments.

While it is true that only a small fraction of Islam's billion-plus adherents are currently radicalized to the point of violence, it is equally as true that a large majority of Muslims do yearn for a world ruled by Sharia Law. This is simply incompatible with both a classically liberal constitutional republic and the very existence of Christianity and Judaism. Mohamed established a permanent state of war between Islam and everyone else, dividing the world into *Dar al Islam* and *Dar al Harb* (the House of War). Fourteen hundred years of clerical decrees by the *Mah'di* interpreting the Hadiths and Koran (and Siyar) have done nothing to temper this worldview.

How many Muslim-run states allow the free practice of other religions? The answer should be as obvious as the nose on one's face, but if a politician or commentator points this out, the Progressives immediately shout them down as being "intolerant" or "Islamaphobic." The irony of their disapprobation is the fact that Progressives will be the first to have their heads lopped off if ever the Mohammedans come to power!

In many ways Modernity is the more dangerous of the two heresies because, as does Lucifer, it mixes lies with the truth, cloaking itself in faux philosophical language and belief structure that virulently attacks our founding fathers and their sound belief structure based in faith and divine providence. In essence, Modernity denies God, nay worse, *mocks* God and all those who express and practice their faith in Him and His natural law. It has insidiously eroded the fabric of American society to the point at which now a school district in Charlotte, North Carolina[3] is considering teaching children that there are no little girls or little boys, but rather an androgynous Gender Unicorn. Had someone twenty years ago (or even ten years ago) told me that this would be discussed anywhere outside the confines of an insane asylum, I would have thought that individual balmy at best. Now, in this insane asylum of modern America, I am made to feel like the inmate. And it is now time for this inmate to begin to fight back and I pray to Almighty God that many of my fellow Americans will join me.

In 2011, after a career that took me from policing the projects in East Baltimore as a cop to being a paratrooper in the 82nd Airborne Division in Operation Desert Storm;

Senior Attorney for the Drug Enforcement Administration; Command Legal Advisor for Special Operations Forces in Iraq and Afghanistan during Operations Iraqi Freedom and Enduring Freedom; and, on faculty at the Army War College, I almost died due to Stage IV Melanoma that had metastasized to my ribs and lungs. At first, I was both frightened and very sad about losing everything here on Earth: my family, career, and my purpose for being. Or, so I thought.

By the Grace of God, the amazing treatment by my oncology team at University of Pennsylvania, the heartfelt prayers of family and friends, and the intercession of our Blessed Mother and a possible Saint named Laurinda Steele Lacey,[4] I was not only spared death, but also given tremendous insight into both my personal redemption[5] and what should be all of our priorities in life. That is to be godly servants to others, from our intimate family and friends to strangers: all who have specific material and spiritual needs.

This "down time" also gave me time to write again. After three books on military and policing (two coauthored with my Special Forces friends Morgan Banks and James Patterson) I now wanted to write about the spiritual state of affairs in America and this temporal life. For in my awakening after near-death, I starkly saw an America I did not recognize from the grand republic of my childhood: from empty churches, citizens not waving at police officers, to not being able to smell the burning leaves of autumn. Seemingly disparate but interrelated freedoms that have been lost to the quickly encroaching nihilism of Modernity.

Perhaps nowhere is this change in America seen more vividly than in the mundane: flying on commercial airliners, for instance. On my first commercial airline flight, an Eastern

Airlines Lockheed Electra turboprop from Baltimore to Louisville in 1968, all the passengers were bathed and dressed nicely. Men were in coat and tie, while the Ladies wore dresses or blouses and skirts. My folks made me wear a bowtie and coat. Even at the age of eight, boys were expected to look and act like gentlemen. The "flight attendants" were all attractive women and were called "stewardesses." That word was not used as a diminutive or pejorative: it was their job and they did it with pride and a heck of a lot more efficiently and pleasantly than nowadays. Flight attendants, like officious functionaries and senior noncommissioned officers in every army, have that special ability to say, "Sir," with such inflection that they might as well be saying, "Idiot" or worse. And, getting handed a Styrofoam cup containing four ounces of burnt coffee by a male flight attendant, who is most likely indifferent to women, is not nearly as special as getting served a hot meal and a complementary mixed drink by a polite and attractive stewardess.

As an adult, I often have to fly with a sidearm, and no longer being in a job that allows me to carry a weapon in the passenger compartment, I must lock my weapons in checked baggage. Airline ticket agents "inspect" my weapons prior to their being locked inside locked Pelican cases. This rigmarole reminds me of what one of my former Army commanders, Major General Gary L. Harrell, used to say about "a hog looking at a wristwatch." Most ticket agents, while pleasant enough, would not have known which end of the barrel was the muzzle or breech, moreover whether the weapon was loaded or not. Nonetheless, we go through this charade in order to keep us all "safe." Unarmed, but safe: truly an oxymoron.

And, what difference would it make anyway? I thought not for the first time, paraphrasing that hateful woman ("She who must not be named"). Most people, educated by Hollywood, falsely believed that (1) loaded weapons could somehow magically fire without someone sticking their booger hooker on the trigger, and (2) an aircraft would catastrophically decompress if, by chance, a 9 mm hole somehow unlikely managed to pierce the plane's outer skin. The reality is much less dramatic. Pressurized air would slowly leak from the plane and, if the aircraft's pressurization system could not keep up with the leakage (again unlikely), the pilot would still have plenty of time to descend below 15,000 feet where oxygen was not so scarce. No one would get sucked out of the plane as depicted in the bombing sequence in *Airport* and many films since.

Making my way through insanely long TSA "security" lines, I have often had other, darker thoughts. If I hear one more person say, "Well, at least it makes us safe," as justification for complete strangers pawing through our belongings and seizing nail clippers from our carry-on bags, I will scream. Ben Franklin once said, "He who sacrifices freedom for security deserves neither." Americans witness this truism in action *every* time we take to the not-so-friendly skies. If we are forced to endure this ignominy, then the terrorists have won. Period. Why did we military volunteers, including many friends who were grievously wounded or killed, fight in the so-called global war on terrorism if this is the reward we come home to see? Plain and simple, the Muj have won if we are paying others to treat us with such disdain.

Of all the relatively few *really* bad decisions George W. Bush made as President of the United States, the creation of the Department of Homeland Security and its subordinate agency, Transportation Security Administration (TSA), had to be one of the worst. Despite the Hollywood scriptwriters' attempts to hide the truth, *All in the Family's* Archie Bunker was spot-on when commenting on many social issues, including the hijacking scourge of the early seventies when he said, ""You wanna stop airline skyjacking, all you gotta do is give all of the passengers guns."

Even if the gun hating/fearing factions objected to giving every good folk a firearm, just issuing everyone a nightstick or a sap would make much more sense than making everyone a potential victim by disarming them. And, if we just did what El Al (Israel's airline) does, which is to profile suspects rather than humiliate octogenarians, Catholic sisters, veterans, and law-abiding citizens, we would be safer and freer than we are now. Why is this so difficult to see? While I have met some genuinely good and hard working TSA agents, it appears to all but the blind and retarded that TSA is nothing more than a gigantic workfare for many sick, lame, and lazy in our big city airports like Atlanta and Chicago. In return, they abuse their authority by frisking folks like my friends and me . . . folks you *want* on your side if things go sideways on a flight.

Perhaps I am just getting old and cranky and should not fight the inevitable. But then a fellow traveler, anxious to stuff all of his worldly possessions into the aircraft's tiny overhead bin, jostles me out of that lie. What was that word for where people saw different eras as somehow better, more civilized and less violent than their own? My passions are something deeper than plain old *nostalgia*. Some folks hear a song from their youth or smell a home-cooked meal that triggers brief flashes of their past, but my memories and recollections from different periods of my life all point to a pending doom for the republic for which I have fought to protect for most of my adult life.

Men were masculine back then and "gay" was a mood, not a euphemism for a queer. One of my friends, an F-14 Tomcat driver, call sign "Coconut," once commented at a warfighter conference in Little Creek about the "Pussification" of America's fighting forces. "Feminization" may be a nicer way of stating that truth, but American males are being turned into wimps by helicopter moms and public school systems devoid of God and teachers like of School Sisters of Notre Dame.[6] Now, instead of learning to be resilient, students protest to the Progressive zero-tolerance *Mafiosi* about micro-aggressions and grades other than an *A*.

Everyone laughed at the time, but Coconut's words were prophetic. How else could we have been at war with radical Islamists since 2001 and still be standing in long lines at airports and enduring multiple attacks on our home soil without even naming the enemy? The Muj are winning because we have become spiritually and physically weak. We have lost our will while the enemy hones his hatchets.

America and Britain defeated Nazi Germany and Imperial Japan in a third of the time we have been messing around with these half-witted Mohammedans. And, the Square Heads and Japs of World War II could really fight . . . what is wrong with the West nowadays? Where are the twenty-first century's version of the eighth century's Charles Martel (Battle of Tours) or his seventeenth century successor in the fight against Mohammedans, Jan Sobieski (Siege of Vienna)? Or, even the twentieth century's Chesty Puller or Alvin York?

At the senior political level, we haven't had a president with brains and guts in the White House since Ronald Reagan. Perhaps, with Donald Trump, we do. With Barack Obama ensconced there, for eight years if one could believe American voters were that stupid, I routinely found myself rooting for foreign leaders like Bibi Netanyahu instead of America's "Dear Leader." I even felt more kinship with that Commie son of a bitch Vladimir Putin over Barack Hussein Obama. I *never* thought that would happen. As much as I disliked Jimmy Carter's and Bill Clinton's politics, I would still come to attention and greet either of them with, "Good morning Mr. President," if they came into the room. If Barack Hussein Obama walked into that room, the only reason I would stand would be to leave as fast as possible to avoid knocking his Chiclets down his throat. In fact, I blotted out his name with a Sharpie on my military retirement certificate and handwrote Ronald Wilson Reagan's name in its stead.

When I met Clinton at a private party in 1997, Bill was still on crutches from an injury sustained after stumbling at professional golfer Greg Norman's house in Florida (at least that was the official story of how he sustained his injury). I was standing in the chow line at the catered event and was surprised when I turned around and saw the President in line right behind me. "Hi, I'm Bill Clinton," POTUS said, extending his hand. I almost exclaimed, "No S---," before quickly composing and introducing myself.

I then observed Bill Clinton work the catering line, talking with the workers and enjoying himself. I was impressed because, even though on crutches from a fall at Greg Norman's house, Clinton served himself. Moreover, there was no press at the event, so there was no political capital to be gained. Bill Clinton sincerely seemed to like people. Not so much so with Hillary. Back at the tables, I noticed Mizzzz Rodham sitting with a stare on her puss that could freeze Satan, as Secret Service agents served her meal. Servitude is a forbidden concept to true leaders; apparently not so much to the creature that Progressives proclaimed as the smartest woman in the world.

Whatever my opinions of the Clintons, nothing they did yet ever sank as low personally or professionally as Obama. I have formed two contrasting mental images: one, of Ronald Reagan and Her Majesty Queen Elizabeth II horseback riding at Windsor Castle; and, the other of the former occupant of 1600 Pennsylvania Avenue dressed in some ridiculous Oriental outfit bowing to a foreign potentate in China. Ronald Reagan, or my dad for that matter, never *bowed* to another man. Barack Hussein Obama always seems to be doing so. But, the American people made that bed and the so-called opposition party was not too different. It was only the flavor of their Kool-Aid that differed, as both parties seemed incapable of fiscal restraint or virtuous living. I feel as if I am witnessing the end of Christendom and the more recent dream of America's Founding Fathers.

This tome is a collection of vignettes, seemingly disparate but all with a thread winding through them that gainsays both radical Islam and Modernity and all of their false promises. It astounds me that we had a viable Democratic candidate that is a confessed Socialist. "It will work if we only try harder," as university professors and the media have brainwashed dimwitted high school students, teachers, school bus drivers and Millennials into believing such rubbish. Hitler, Stalin, Mao and Pol Pot, as well as countless minor potentates in sub-Saharan Africa, killed over 120 million people in the twentieth century trying really hard to make it work. How many millions will the Progressives send to the gulags to make it work this time?

Think I am joking? As I write, there are diverse federal and state prosecutors scheming to imprison people for being

Climate Change "deniers." Climate Change fanatics, Green Parties and all of Progressivism are simply filling the vacuum left when we allowed governments to take God out of schools and our social discourse. The human soul yearns to believe in our Creator and when society squelches that yearning, it is quite natural for man to fall into the worship of modern-day Baals: drugs, doing it "My Way," Climate Change, Animal Rights, LBGTQ, and all the other lies of Progressivism.

I want to thank our founding fathers, among them George Washington, Charles Carroll of Carrollton (the only Roman Catholic signer of the Declaration of Independence), Thomas Jefferson, James Madison, Benjamin Franklin, John Adams, and Patrick Henry. Also, it is oft forgotten the disproportionate sacrifice of the small minority of Jews in America. In Georgia, the first patriot to be killed was a Jew, Francis Salvador.

The most important of the financiers of our Revolution was Haym Salomon, who lent his fortune and then some to the Continental Congress. In the last days of the war, Salomon advanced the American government $200,000. He was never paid back and died in bankruptcy. Contrary to the Progressive drivel that passes for a basic education in America, these men are not, as some have claimed, dead old white men and slave owners, who could not foresee the advent of computers, airplanes, and the Internet. Rather, they were geniuses that understood the fundamental and enduring nature of mankind. Many were polyglots and most were voracious readers and correspondents.

The Constitution is a pact between free peoples and their government. It confers limited powers to that government, but confers nothing to the individual. The Bill of Rights merely *acknowledges* what are God-given rights under the natural law: rights to freely associate with those we chose; the right to be armed for defense against bandits and an oppressive government; the right to be free from unfettered search and seizure; and, all the rights enumerated and more. If the Second Amendment were repealed tomorrow, it would not change one iota the inherent right I possess to arm myself in a fashion similar to the way soldiers are armed.

Now, I watch as the new Soviets disinter the graves of Confederate heroes; unilaterally and without referendum take out decades-old beautiful stained glass from the National Cathedral because it "offends" the ignorant; and, plague the populace with so many laws and regulations that the average person can unknowingly commit *Three Felonies a Day*.[7]

I pray that we can turn our republic around before it is too late to restore so many lost freedoms. Author John Ross, in his 1996 book *Unintended Consequences,* speaks of how to boil a frog. One of his protagonists explains that if you put a frog into a pan of boiling water, it will quickly hop out. But, if you place it into a pan of cool water, then slowly raise the temperature of the water to boiling, the frog will cook to death. We, The People, are being slowly boiled to death by ever more intrusive laws and taxes. A government that was created for We, The People has grown far outside the bounds set up as safety nets to limit its size, growth, and reach. In my home state of Delaware, the largest employer is the State of Delaware! Such a self-licking ice cream cone cannot last. Sooner or later, socialists will run out of other peoples' money to spend. I also pray in earnest that America quickly wakes up to what is happening to them and our country. If not, it may be "Time to feed the hogs" (another allusion to *Unintended Consequences*).

The first section of the book deals with the threat of Islam. It is not a new threat, as any rigorous student of history can tell you. Churchill wisely stated in regards to India in the mid-Twentieth Century, "While the Hindu elaborates his argument, the Muslim sharpens his sword."[8] The West has been at war with the *Mujahedeen* (Muj) since the seventh century. The Muj know it, but the West of Modernity willfully ignores it. When Europe figures out its plans on dealing with its Fifth Column Muj, funded by Saudi Arabia and their willing dupes at the UN, it might be too late to prevent "Eurabia" from destroying Europe's culture and priceless art and churches. But, I hold out hope that there is still enough of the old European blood not spilled in the trenches of WWI or the fronts of WWII coursing through the veins of this generation that they will wake up in time to save Christendom from the ravages of the new caliphate.

But, unless we get our own house in order and return to a community bound together by the common virtues of our Judeo-Christian monotheistic faith, we will lose the battle with Islam. America's woes today can be directly attributable to the selfish Me generation of which I am partially to blame. Rather than keeping our churches full, the Boy Scouts a safe and wholesome organization to teach boys to become men, and, our personal lives virtuous, we will be nearly caved in by the true evil of Modernity that Orwell, Churchill, and Chesterton warned us about. "When Man ceases to worship God he does not worship nothing but worships everything."[9] We must all become Saint Thomas More, a speaker of the truth no matter the costs, and do not be a gossip, whisperer, and rumormonger as so many of our military and political managers (vice leaders) have become.

Note: A word about word choice. While I recognize that the use of gratuitously foul language is the sign of a weak mind and intemperate spirit, I concurrently recognize that most Americans, to include my beloved soldiers, sailors, airmen and Marines, do not speak like Hilaire Belloc or William F Buckley Jr. Therefore, when appropriate, I use the language of the trenches and fields of battle. A Pashtun fighter will be called a Muj or, as I have done already, an Arab Islamist may be called *Haji* or other term of endearment. If it offends you, either get over it or ignore it. I will not bend to Fascism in the guise of political correctness. Lastly, I organized these vignettes into two books, the second book, Modernity, focuses on the battle that we must first win if we ever wish to defeat the Muj in the long run.

David G. Bolgiano
Wilmington, Delaware

BOOK ONE
THE MOHAMMEDANS

CHAPTER ONE

THE EXISTENTIAL
THREAT OF ISLAM

H istory is a funny thing. Far too many people "two-dimensionalize" those not of their generation, creating cartoon-like characters out of complex individuals: evil ones like Stalin and Hitler; and, good people like Churchill and Reagan. And, in so doing, they diminish the threat of a modern people's determined to wipe off the face of the map Jews, Christians, Hindus, atheists and homosexuals.[1] It amazes me how the Western media turns a blind eye to the atrocities committed under the *Dar al-Islam* (House of Islam), yet vilifies the Jews in Israel for acting in righteous self-defense. Even in so-called "moderate" Turkey, Muslim leaders who call for religious tolerance, recognition of Israel, and advances in scientific knowledge, are similarly vilified and even persecuted. Turkey's President Erdogan used a fake coup to round up tens of thousands of dissenters. The result is a Turkey more Islamic and less secular than the country Ataturk envisioned.

For instance, Muhammed Gülen, founder of the Hizmet movement, lived in a self-imposed exile in Pennsylvania for fear of persecution in Turkey. Gülen taught an Anatolian version of Islam, derived from Sunni Muslim scholar Said Nursî's teachings. Hizmet followers believe in science, interfaith dialogue among the People of the Book (Christians, Jews, and Muslims), and multi-party democracy. They have initiated dialogue with the Vatican and even some Jewish organizations. This is intolerable to radical Islamists in Turkey, who seem to be on a rage throughout their caliphate and are now threatening Europe and the entire West as well. Not surprisingly, Erdogan, the same small-minded leader that attempted to sue a German cartoon artist for an unflattering rendering, blames Gülen for the attempted coup and is demanding the US extradite this man back to Turkey.

Further lost on many Westerners today are those acts of Islamic brutality committed in earlier centuries. Contrary to the revisionists history taught in most universities today, the Crusades were not an evil, oppressive act committed by plundering elites, but rather a direct response to the violent Muslim incursions into the Holy Land, Levant and the Maghreb. Most Americans are completely ignorant of the 1,400-year onslaught of Islam against the West and the heroes who defended our way of life. A very few might be familiar with Charles "The Hammer" Martel's defense of France at the Battle of Tours in AD 732 or Jan Sobieski's valiant and amazing defeat of an Ottoman Turk[2] army three times larger than his at the Battle of Vienna in AD 1683 , but most are woefully ignorant of anything more remote than their last debit card expenditure at McDonald's. This is a huge mistake, for it prevents us from discerning real threats in our own times. Scholars of the strategic arts called it the "inability to think while in the blender." It can also be called just plain *willful* ignorance. But when folks chose to be intentionally ignorant, like Europeans turning a blind eye to the threat posed by radical Islam in their own backyards, such ignorance is not only criminally negligent, but also poses an existential threat. Hence, these dupes become Fifth Columnists for Islam.

Most of Europe has stripped its citizens of their God-given right of self-defense (Switzerland being an obvious exception because of their requirement that all able-bodied adult citizens remain armed with assault rifles as members of the militia) and true free speech. In England, Sweden, Germany, and Holland, politicians and writers who speak out in truth against the cancer of Sharia law are fined and imprisoned. Ironically, this is done in the name of so-called *tolerance*. George Orwell's *newspeak* is upon us. Sadly, most in America are content to live with the bread and circuses of pop TV as Rome burns. But an enemy within, homegrown Radical Islam, as well as all of its derivatives such as Prislam (those being recruited throughout America's prison system by radicalized Imams brought in as prison chaplains).and Louis Farrakhan's Nation of Islam, threatens all of us personally as well as the loveliness and sanctity of our Christian churches and Jewish synagogues. Europe is just beginning to wake up to the warning calls of the few wise men and women with the courage to blast through the wall of ignorance funded by the oil sheiks and built by the politically correct in European and American academia. And, predictably, the complicit mainstream media is already marginalizing those that are wise to these threats as "extremists" and "far right-wing" elements.

When these Muslim evildoers shoot up Paris, San Bernardino, and Orlando, Progressives scream about so-called gun violence as if inanimate objects, firearms, rather than individuals are responsible for this carnage. First, gun violence is neither good nor evil. I have personally used gun violence to stop armed robbery here in America and to kill enemies on foreign soil. So, intelligent people must stop using language the Left has written for us. Terrorists, not guns, killed all the victims at the sites herein. And, if one Parisian or one Niçois in France, or one homosexual in Orlando was armed and properly trained, there is a good chance the Muj would have been killed before spilling so much innocent blood.

This threat has long been recognized by the Roman Catholic Church, yet has been ignored by most of the priests that are products of the felt-banner Catholicism of the 60s. The truth is powerful medicine against this threat as so presciently stated by Father George William Rutler, a Roman Catholic priest and the pastor of the Church of St. Michael in Manhattan:

After another devastating ISIS attack in France, this time against a priest in his 80s while he was saying Mass, the answer isn't just, "Do nothing." As racism distorts race and sexism corrupts sex, so does pacifism affront peace. Turning the other cheek is the counsel Christ gave in the instance of an individual when morally insulted: humility conquers pride. It has nothing to do with self-defense.

The Catholic Church has always maintained that the defiance of an evil force is not only a right, but an obligation. Its Catechism (cf. #2265) cites St. Thomas Aquinas, "Legitimate defense can be not only a right but a grave duty for someone responsible for another's life, the common good of the family or of the State."

A father is culpable if he does not protect his family. A bishop has the same duty as a spiritual father of his sons and daughters in the church, just as the civil state has as its first responsibility the maintenance of the "tranquility of order" through self-defense.

Christ warned the apostles, as shepherds, to beware of wolves. This requires both the "shrewdness of serpents and the innocence of doves." To shrink from the moral duty to protect peace by not using force when needed is to be innocent as a serpent and shrewd as a dove. That is not innocence; it is naiveté.

Saint John Capistrano led an army against the Moors in 1456 to protect Belgrade. In 1601, Saint Lawrence of Brindisi did the same in defense of Hungary. As Franciscans, they carried no sword and charged on horseback into battle carrying a crucifix. They inspired the shrewd generals and soldiers, whom they had assembled through artful diplomacy, with their brave innocence.

This is not obscure trivia. Were it not for Charles Martel at Tours in 732 and Jan Sobieski at the gates of Vienna in 1683, and most certainly had Pope Saint Pius V not enlisted Andrea Doria and Don Juan at Lepanto in 1571, we would not be here now. No Western nations as we know them, no universities, no modern science, no human rights would exist.

In the ninth century, the long line of martyrs of Cordoba told the Spanish Umayyad Caliph Abd Ar-Rahman II that his denial of Christ was infernal, and that they would rather die than surrender. Saint Juan de Ribera (d. 1611) and Saint Alfonsus Liguori (d. 1787) repeated the admonition that the concept of peace in Islam requires not coexistence but submission.

The dormancy of Islam until recent times, however, has obscured the threat that this poses, especially to a Western civilization that has grown flaccid in virtue and ignorant of its own moral foundations. The shortcut to handling the crisis is to deny that it exists. On the first day of the Democratic National Convention in Philadelphia, there were over sixty speeches, and yet not one of them mentioned ISIS.

Vice has destroyed countless individual souls, but in the decline of civilizations, weakness has done more harm than vice. "Peace for our time" is as empty now as it was when Chamberlain went to Munich and honor was bartered in Vichy.

Hilaire Belloc, who knew Normandy and all of Europe well, said in 1929, "We shall almost certainly have to reckon with Islam in the near future. Perhaps, if we lose our faith, it will rise. For after this subjugation of the Islamic culture by the nominally Christian had already been achieved, the political conquerors of that culture began to notice two disquieting features about it. The first was that its spiritual foundation proved immovable; the second, that its area of occupation did not recede, but on the contrary slowly expanded."

The priest in Saint-Étienne-du-Rouvrary in Normandy, France, was not the first to die at the altar, and he will not be the last. In his old age, the priest embodied a civilization that has been betrayed by a generation whose hymn was John Lennon's "Imagine," that there was neither heaven nor hell but "above us only sky" and "all the people living for today." When reality intrudes, they can only leave teddy bears and balloons at the site of a carnage they call "inexplicable."

I am not one prone to leaving teddy bears or balloons. Instead, my friends and I would rather leave a trail of dead Mohammedans from France to Mecca. But first, we need to educate the populace or else we end up being lone wolves tilting at windmills, as we were in Operations Enduring and Iraqi Freedom. Had we been given the authority to kill bad guys that our parents and grandparents had in WWII, al Qaeda and ISIS would have been totally destroyed. Instead, as discussed in later chapters, we spend more time and energy worrying about "collateral damage," "nation-building" and prosecuting our own for silly rules violations than we did killing bad guys. As one of my former commanders presciently observed, "At first I thought maybe the COIN (counterinsurgency) fight was the right way to go, but at some point maybe we should have tried the other way!"

To learn more about the real dangers of Islam and what we lay people can do to confront its lies, I commend all of Brigitte Gabriel's books[3] and material from ACT for America. As one who grew up amongst the violence of the Mohammedans in Lebanon, she so eloquently explains the problems facing Christendom. We either beat them back into their minor caliphate stone-age lands (and take their oil by force if necessary) *now* or deal with this fatal cancer later. Why not now?

CHAPTER TWO

FOURTEEN CENTURIES
OF IMBECILES ARE ENOUGH!

In the 1927 Supreme Court case of *Buck v. Bell*, Justice Oliver Wendell Holmes penned the (in)famous lines, "Three generations of imbeciles are enough." While speaking of a statute to sterilize a feeble-minded and promiscuous woman, the facts of *Buck* are horrific. But, there is an underlying truth of Holmes' words when applied to a radical, violent, and incompatible religion that Islam has consistently shown itself to be. Here is just some of its spawn:

- Rabid anti-Semitism that figuratively and literally wishes to wipe Israel off the face of the Earth;

- An honor-killing society that willfully, knowingly and with moral sanction lies to all it considers "infidels" (I.e., anyone not a Muslim);

- A pathological jealously and hatred of the successes of the West. I know, I have heard about how wonderful the Arab was at Algebra . . . blah, blah, blah. Truth in fact, the Mohammedan invaders of Spain learned much more from the Christians and Jews there than vice versa. Furthermore, what, other than war, famine, and blood feuds, has this "religion of peace" brought to the world?

Violent extremism follows wherever they land. And, when they don't quite have enough of a majority to lord over the dhimmitude, they make Al Sharpton and Jesse Jackson look like amateurs at playing the race card. The Council for American Islamic Relations (CAIR) did not do squat to condemn the 9/11 terror attacks. In fact, most of its members were cheering from high-rises in Falls Church, Virginia, and Jersey City, New Jersey. But, CAIR was there to immediately whine that our law enforcement and intelligence community was "targeting" Muslims. It worked. The US Army fired a seasoned warrior and scholar, Lieutenant Colonel Matt Dooley, for daring to query, "Is Islam compatible with a Jeffersonian Democracy?" and the Department of Defense made Koranic scholar and Arabic speaker Major Stephen Coughlin persona non grata because he dared to speak the truth about what the Koran actually says.

Once they hit about 15 percent of the population, "no-go zones" pop up, where police are prohibited or afraid to go. This has already occurred in Paris, Antwerp, and parts of England. And, like lambs to slaughter, off the meek go. Perhaps Western Europe lost too much of its manhood in World War I and World War II. Now, left with wimps afraid of confrontation or being accused of being Islamaphobic (a wise thing to be in light of the existential threat posed by these savages); Old Europe may be too late to save. Unless they dig deep and find the courage to throw the likes of Angela Merkel out of office, Europeans as we know and love them may be gone forever. Europe will become Eurabia.

To us Crusaders at heart and in deed, it seems insane that the United States is supporting Turkey, while we leave little Armenia, the first Christian nation, to seek military support and solace from Vladmir Putin's Russia. Yet, this is not the first time in recent history a Democratic-controlled White House supported the wrong side in the region. The Clinton administration supported Mohammedans in Kosovo, going so far as to bomb Belgrade and further south defile the sacred ground of an earlier battle that took place on 15 June 1389 between a Christian army led by Serbian Prince Lazar Hrebeljanović against the invading Muj armies of the Ottoman Empire.

There is an unfortunate false historical narrative being played out in Western academics and its halls of political power that suggest that the Mohammedans are always the victims of Christian and Jewish oppression. A brief, knowing study of history proves something quite the contrary. Remember, the Crusades were a *reaction* to the violent and virulent spread of Islam from Arabia. In a short century, starting hundreds of years of misery after Mohammed's death, his cancerous tribal "religion of peace" spread at the point of the spear until it encompassed all the lands of Persia, Arabia, the Levant, the Maghreb, Portugal, and Spain. Only countless struggles, bookmarked by the Battle of Tours in 732 and the Vienna in 1683 saved the West, to include all its genius of the likes of Descartes, Michelangelo, Shakespeare, Vivaldi, Bach, Brahms, Beethoven, and more, from ruin.

Now, due in large part by Saudi largesse and the willful ignorance of progressive politicians, professors, and media, many in Europe and the USA are being taught a false historical narrative. A prime example of such facile beliefs is that which underpins the Boycott-Divest-Sanction (BDS) Israel movement so prevalent on liberal college and university campuses. For more on this, I refer you again to the outstanding work of Brigitte Gabriel. As for Armenia, the most one might learn in high school history class are faint rumblings about an "alleged" genocide, where in fact the Muj put a million Armenian Christians and other non-Muslims to the sword in the early twentieth century. It is not providential to watch most motion pictures made after 1960, with the exception of *Lonesome Dove, Saving Private Ryan,* and most of Clint Eastwood's films, but parents should encourage their children to watch the 2014 movie *The Cut.* It vividly and accurately depicts what Turks (Muslims) did and continue to do to "nonbelievers" in a ruthless and determined fashion.

Perhaps after the attacks in Orlando and San Bernardino, Americans will awaken to the real threat. It ain't gun violence, despite what the *New York Daily News* headline screamed, "Thanks NRA," but rather "Thanks Mohammad!" Remember, gun violence can be a good thing, as when cops use it to quell an armed robbery, homeowners to repel burglars and warriors to kill the enemy in overseas combat operations. Maybe Americans are beginning to figure out the big lie, but do not be too optimistic. Visit any hotel's restaurant or sports bar, where food will often be accompanied by insipid television shows a la truTV and the cretins at the bar will be fixated. Try in vain to ignore the cackling laugh track and guffaws from some of the mouth-breathing patrons. It is impossible not to believe that we have created a bread and circus populace woefully ignorant of an existential threat about to descend upon them.

It may not be tomorrow, but it is coming. Europe has apparently signed its own death warrant as its politicians criminally prosecute prophets like Dutch Parliamentarian Geert Wilders for telling the truth about Islam's obvious goal of creating a worldwide caliphate. And, if the Muj don't get us, perhaps the rabid Left will. If they continue on their current course unchecked, it could take a shooting war to reclaim what are our God-given rights.

But, in the midst of all of this craziness, little Armenia deserves a special place in our hearts and prayers. I met two Armenian army officers that attended a course at the Defense Institute for International Legal Studies (DIILS) in Newport in 2014 and educated their classmates on their nation's plight with Islam. As the Earth's first Christian nation, Armenians know the meaning of suffering. They may just become the twenty-first century's version of Jan Sobieski or Charles Martel. In our own small measure, we can help out by writing and speaking openly about the threat of Islam. And, by staying armed and prepared. Just last Halloween, on a family outing with our grandnephews to a pumpkin ride at a local farm near Philadelphia, 300 burka-clad women poured out of a school bus. Some of them had rather broad shoulders, so we kept at the ready and in front of the kids at all times. These are perilous times and God calls us to be saints and wear His armor.

The good people of Armenia and us Americans are now in a similar predicament. Godspeed to them and I thank God that we may now have a president in power that may finally side with good. With our resources and the will of the warriors amongst us, we might yet again save Christendom and the West.

CHAPTER THREE

BE A MACCABEE: THE URGENCY OF COURAGE IN THE WEST

"Courage is rightly esteemed the first of human qualities (virtues) . . . because it is the quality which guarantees all others"
— WINSTON CHURCHILL.

I n these times of uncertainty, when vacuous television and profane songs rot one's soul, society must dig deep, become full of righteous wrath, and fight back hard against the sins of modernity. We need to manifest courage in our daily lives, political and personal, to fight back against these ills. Nothing less than the fate of the West and our eternal souls are at stake.

Truth, the essence of competence, is the razor-edge sword with which will eviscerate all the lies foisted upon our children: the ultimate denial of God's reign as our creator. America and the greater West are teetering on fiscal, moral, and societal collapse. While faced with a self-declared existential threat in the form of Mohammedanism, these United States and Europe remain preoccupied with their manmade idols such as climate change, sexual preferences, and pornography. The need for steely-eyed courage and righteous wrath is indeed urgent, but our populace remains stymied.

The prayerful and honest men and women now cry out, "Why is this happening?" It is happening because the West has lost its moral compass and soul over the past sixty years. The vision of a moral society set up to counter the evils of National Socialism and Communism has been horrifically blurred. Blessed with an abundance of riches, we have succumbed to the age-old problem: loss of faith. And, to our peril, we ignore history.

For instance, Charles Martel, who helped save Christendom and all the future glories of the Renaissance from the scourge of the Moors invading from Spain in 732, possessed such courage. As did Jan Sobieski, the Polish general who defended Vienna against the Muslim hordes of the Ottoman Empire. These were faithful and courageous men, as were our republic's founders. Now, Europe, lacking the will to even acknowledge such a threat and prosecuting those that do, is slitting its own throat in the process. The West would also serve itself well by reading and learning from Scripture.

In 142 BC, the Maccabees forced the Seleucids to retreat from the Land of Israel after two decades of ferocious fighting. This tribe known as the Maccabees, from the Hebrew word for "hammer" due to the hammer blows they struck against their enemies, freed Israel after more than five hundred years of subjugation. Yet, today, most Western progressives rant about how "the Jews stole the Palestinians' land." While radical Islamists invade Europe, rape women, and decapitate those who do not submit to Sharia law, these useful idiots organize anti-Semitic Boycott-Diversify-Sanction (BDS) movements on supposedly educated university campuses across the United States and Europe. Truth demands that we become modern day Maccabees to stand against these evils. We can cower behind our stick-build walls, scuttle off to Mass to hear lukewarm priests tell us to be nice to each other and welcome Muslims, and buy into the lies of Modernity. Or, we can do solid spiritual activities such as, for a Roman Catholic, attend Tridentine (traditional) Latin Mass, where the focus of the priest and congregation is on God rather than entertaining each other, and become Maccabees.

CHAPTER FOUR

THE AMBUSH OF A PHILADELPHIA POLICE OFFICER - A STUDY IN COURAGE AND COWARDICE

Late on the night of January 7, 2016, Philadelphia Police Officer Jesse Hartnett was patrolling the streets of the city uniformed and in a marked patrol car. Suddenly and unexpectedly, 30-year-old Edward Archer, clothed in a Middle Eastern dish dash robe, ran at Hartnett's vehicle from across the street on Hartnett's left side yelling, "Allah Akbar!" Halfway across the street, Archer raised his arm and began firing eleven rounds from a semi-automatic pistol. Multiple rounds struck Officer Hartnett, yet heroically he had the stamina and moral courage to exit his vehicle and chase Archer down the darkened street. Hartnett fired his duty weapon at the fleeing dangerous suspect, injuring him enough to enable his capture shortly thereafter. Miraculously, Hartnett has survived his wounds, as did Archer.

Officer Hartnett's actions that evening should be held out as a shining example of how a hero operates under stress. Not giving up, even after being shot, he charged after the bad guy instead of hiding in the police vehicle and awaiting medical assistance, neither of which would have been unreasonable or cowardly. In this era where police are targeted for no other reason than being a part of the Thin Blue Line, citizens and fellow officers should loudly applaud Hartnett's bravery and resiliency under fire. Instead, some police chiefs are firing officers who dare to speak out against the evils of Black Lives Matter (BLM) thugs.[1]

Contrasted with such physical and moral courage, the cowardice and infidelity of his political masters is particularly noteworthy. Even after it became clear that Archer's motivations were rooted in radical Islam, both the Mayor Jim Kenney and Police Commissioner Richard Ross Jr. immediately defaulted to the Progressive shibboleth that "Islam is a religion of peace" and "the suspect's criminal acts have nothing to do with Islam." No, Mrs. Cleaver, Archer could have just as easily been a Quaker or Roman Catholic! We all know how those Mormons are always strapping suicide vests on and blowing up buses or the market place.

The second knee-jerk lie these political hacks regurgitated is that gun violence was at fault here. Oh, never mind the fact that Officer Hartnett was shot with a stolen police weapon; to so-called Progressives, guns are the root of this problem, not radicalized Muslims or graduates of Prislam. This constant tendency to deflect blame from individuals to an inanimate instrumentality is the hallmark of Progressivism. It is radicalized Muslims and criminal thugs that are the threat to free Americans, not guns. Guns are our first line of defense from terrorists, thugs, and a tyrannical government.

America, and to a greater degree Europe, is under assault by an enemy that has never attempted to hide their goals. Usama bin Laden clearly stated the goals of al Qaeda over twenty years ago. Muslim Brotherhood leader Qutb stated his goals in very clearly writing from prison in Egypt in the 60s. Muslims cheer and await the return of domination over the West, a new caliphate bent on subjugating or killing nonbelievers. To those who pooh-pooh this truth I state, "Show me a Muslim ruled nation that tolerates free exercise of other religions or even free speech and I will show you a hog that flies."

It is time for some Hartnett-like tactical courage, like that shown by our warriors in Iraq and Afghanistan at the tip of the spear, to be exercised by our strategic leaders. If Philadelphia's mayor is any barometer, that courage will not be found in the Democratic Party. And, if John McCain and Lindsey Graham are the litmus of the Republican Party, the GOP is damned as well.

Then-candidate Donald Trump gave a marvelous nomination acceptance speech that rivaled the Gipper. Then, a few weeks later, he took the gloves off with a speech that made me scream, "Finally!" He came out swinging against the twin evils of Barack Hussein Obama and Hillary Rodham Clinton:

Obama-Clinton have single-handedly destabilized the Middle East, handed Iraq, Libya and Syria to ISIS, and allowed our personnel to be slaughtered at Benghazi. Then they put Iran on the path to nuclear weapons. Then they allowed dozens of veterans to die waiting for medical care that never came.

Hillary Clinton put the whole country at risk with her illegal email server, deleted evidence of her crime, and lied repeatedly about her conduct which endangered us all" They released criminal aliens into our country who killed one innocent American after another—like Sarah Root and Kate Steinle—and have repeatedly admitted migrants later implicated in terrorism.

They have produced the worst recovery since the Great Depression. They have shipped millions of our best jobs overseas to appease their global special interests. They have betrayed our security and our workers, and Hillary Clinton has proven herself unfit to serve in any government office.

She is reckless with her emails, reckless with regime change, and reckless with American lives. Our nation has been humiliated abroad and compromised by radical Islam brought onto our shores. We need change now.[2]

Trump hit his stride and finally took off the gloves in this most important presidential race of my lifetime, including Reagan's crucial victory over Carter in 1980. Since 1981, I have served as a peace officer and in the military, including multiple combat tours against Islamists. My duties included stints working in some of our republic's most sensitive counter-terror units, including those preparing cases before the Foreign Intelligence Surveillance Act (FISA) courts. I have also prosecuted and defended criminal suspects from petit thieves to murderers. Something has always set off my "Spidey sense" about both Obama and Clinton, and for years I have felt exactly what Trump said that day.

In my opinion, Barack Obama is not only the worst president in our republic's history, but he is, at best, a Fifth Columnist and, at worst, a Mohammedan Manchurian Candidate. How else can one explain his systemic dismantling of the finest military the world has known by forcing the homosexual-transgender agenda down our throats; wholesale

importation of unvetted Muj and criminals from the Middle
East and Mexico; his willfully ignoring the principles of our
Constitution (in fact, sneering at our founding fathers and all
the goodness they wrought); drastically cutting our nuclear
triad to dangerously low levels; fomenting discord and hatred
by never missing an opportunity to fan the embers of racism;
and, stabbing Israel in the back by giving Iran nukes and
snubbing her leaders. His parting shot of allowing the UN
Security Council to sanction Israel for its building settlements
on the West Bank (land it fought hard for in the Six Day War
of 1967) was particularly cruel and despicable. Israel is the only
democracy and non-Muslim nation in the Levant. Perhaps this
is what motivated Obama.

CHAPTER FIVE

THE DEPARTMENT OF DEFENSE'S INSULTING MESSAGE CONCERNING VICTIMS OF TERRORISM IN SAN BERNARDINO

Just when one thought the Obama administration could not have done anything more treacherous to subvert our ongoing war against Islamic terrorism, here is this little gem from the Department of Defense (DoD) that sickeningly embedded anti-gun rhetoric in its order to our forces to fly the colors at half-mast for the victims of the San Bernardino terror attack:

******

1 As A Mark Of Respect For The Victims Of Gun Violence Perpetrated On December 2, 2015, In San Bernardino, California, And In Accordance With The Presidential Proclamation Of December 2, 2015, The Flag Of The United States Shall Be Flown At Half-Staff Until Sunset, Monday, December 7, 2015.

2   The Flag Shall Be Flown At Half-Staff On All
     Department Of Defense Buildings, Grounds, And
     Naval Vessels Throughout The United States And
     Abroad.

Released By: Michael L. Bruhn, DoD Executive Secretary

******

Note how the Pentagon couches this attack, which by clear and convincing evidence was perpetrated by two Islamic extremists, as victims of "gun violence" rather than murder. Not victims of terrorism, but of gun violence. Why DoD could not have simply said, "Out of respect for those murdered on Dec 2, 2015," and leave the politics out, points to the depths at which Barack Obama and his cronies would sink in order to promulgate his ridiculous anti-firearms agenda. With gun sales at an all-time high and a great majority of Americans showing respect and support the plain meaning of our Second Amendment, this man continued in his rapacious attempt to destroy every vestige of self-reliance in our culture.

But, perhaps more insidious to our soldiers, sailors, airmen and Marines is the hidden message that gun violence is *always* bad. To the contrary, gun violence is not always bad. It would appear that DOD would understand this more than most agencies, as our the law enforcement officers saved more innocent folks from being murdered used gun violence to kill the radical Islamists that perpetrated this act of domestic terrorism. And, tens of millions of citizens peaceably own firearms in the event that they might need to resort to so-called gun violence in a lawful act of defense of self or others. Even more disturbingly, one might conclude that this message,

DOD'S INSULT OF TERROR VICTIMS

intentional or not, honors the terrorists themselves as they were also killed by gun violence.

As veterans of multiple combat tours and as law enforcement officers, my friends and I have used gun violence on diverse occasions in the performance of our duties, and, as citizens, we are always prepared to protect our family and ourselves with gun violence, Like most rational, law-abiding citizens, we see firearms as tools. To imbue some evil animus to an inanimate object is simply deflecting personal responsibility from the individual; which, is exactly what Democrats and their Progressive ideology is all about.

Barack Obama became so tone deaf to the voice of America that he attempted to use victims of terror in America to squarely place the blame for such violence in the laps of the warriors and citizens who wish to protect and serve the Republic. During his lame duck year in office, it is clear that he pulled out all the stops in his efforts to harm our Constitutional Republic. It is very sad that his coterie of political appointees and the spineless flag officers in the Pentagon became aiders and abettors his villainy.

CHAPTER SIX

WHY THE WEST MIGHT
LOSE ITS WAR WITH ISLAM

After Islamists murdered approximately one hundred persons and grievously wounded an equal number in and around Paris, that country went into a panic, locking down its populace and scrambling to make sense of evil. One leader said she is "Deeply shaken." Another, "Shocked." The same "shocked and deeply shaken" response followed the murder of eighty-nine persons in Nice on Bastille Day 2016. But, the French still do nothing to displace and expel the Mohammedan cancer that is killing their nation. In the heart of what was once known as Christendom, police officers now refuse to go into entire Parisian neighborhoods that residents have declared no-go zones for non-Muslims.

Sadly, thirty days later, France, the EU, and most of America was back to sipping the Starbuck's coffee and playing golf or Xbox, because we seem to lack the will to eradicate this scourge from our free and democratic societies. Yet, unless we take immediate and unfettered action, this enemy will slit our throats one by one as we bleat our protests to those who do not care. It is time for war, yet we seem to have forgotten how to wage it.

A just and rigorous theory of war is rooted in two principles: national interest must retain its primacy over the collective goals of the international community; and, that self-defense, individual, collective, or anticipatory, must be the cause of any use of force. From these principles, America should gauge the scope, amount, and duration of its application of military force necessary to reach its enduring goals of security, prosperity and preservation of American values rooted in our Constitution.[1]

Once this theory of war is clearly stated and acted upon, both our adversaries and our allies will know our intent and resolve. The desired result is a not so fragile peace and a more secure world marketplace for commerce, ideas, and freedom. The time has come to publicly identify our enemy, radical Islam and all those who support it, and then get about the business of mercilessly hunting them out, root and branch, from our society.

It is unconscionable that radical Islamists are controlling areas of Paris, France; Malmo, Sweden; and, now, cities in America. It is unconscionable that Orlando occurred *after* the suspect was on the FBI's radar. Their so-called religion is incompatible with a constitutional republic or any other form of civil democracy. There, it is said. And, I mean it. Having served in multiple combat tours in Southwest Asia and seeing friends and colleagues killed and maimed, I am tired of seeing such sacrifice without our political leadership giving the military workable and effective rules of engagement designed to kill a clearly determined foe. And, I am tired of pretending Islam is just another flavor of monotheism.

Three Regimental Combat Teams (if they still exist), supported by close air support elements enjoying air supremacy, could literally wipe ISIS off the face of the Earth in Syria and

Iraq. Yet, even in the face of an existential threat against our way of life, we seem more concerned about appeasing the ICRC, Amnesty International, and other Progressive Internationalists over human rights laws. These are the same evil cabal of Globalists that vilifies nationalism and mocks Americans as "cowboys."

I wish we had more cowboys, because it is cowboy nationalism that gives us both the will and legal authority to fight. Sun Tzu, in his *The Art of War*, observed that national unity was an essential requirement of victorious war. If America cedes its core values to a conglomerate of diverse international interests, we risk diminishing our power and sovereignty to the point of becoming, like France, a second-tier voice in a parliamentary aggregate slouching toward mediocrity: easy targets for Islamists. Yet, all the Globalists such as Angela Merkel and the EU's leadership can muster is a bleat to allow more Syrians, Yemenis, Algerians, Libyans and other Muslims into our lands.

Even in the face of a sea of Islamic horror shows here and abroad, these Globalists continue to decry nationalism and are stridently pushing America to the brink of subservience to the United Nations or some similar supernumerary force. This *must* not happen. Winston Churchill, so despised by Barack Obama, was the twentieth century's greatest politician in time of war. He correctly valued nationalism, saying, "If you will not fight for right when you can easily win without blood shed; if you will not fight when your victory is sure and not too costly; you may come to the moment when you will have to fight with all the odds against you and only a precarious chance of survival. There may even be a worse case. You may have to fight when there is no hope of victory, because it is better to perish than to live as slaves.

One ought never to turn one's back on a threatened danger and try to run away from it. If you do that, you will double the danger. But if you meet it promptly and without flinching, you will reduce the danger by half. Never run away from anything. Never! Do not let spacious plans for a new world divert your energies from saving what is left of the old.

Accordingly, a decade and a half after 9/11, it is finally time for the United States of America to declare war against a committed, known, and declared enemy: Radical Islam. They have no problem identifying themselves. Usama bin Laden laid it all out in his fatwas against the West long before 9/11. It is political folly, insanity, or misdirection to call this threat by any other name. This war has been raging hot and cold since the seventh century. It is time to extinguish it for good, at least in the regions we continue to hold. Seventeenth century Vienna had General Sobieski to come to its rescue against the Islamic Ottoman Turks. Now, in the early decades of the twenty-first century, it is a little bit more than disconcerting that our political leaders are arming Iran with nuclear weapons and allowing tens of thousands of Islamists inside our borders.

We need a Jan Sobieski. Sadly, observing the empty pews of most European and American churches, it is doubtful such a person of character still exists in the West. But they are out there and *you* might be one of them. These are times for saints to stand up and be counted. Forget about your precious SF-86[2] (security clearance form) if doing the right thing means shouting these warnings from the highest mountaintops. If we cower now from the PC bullyboys, what good will we be when the chips are down and the savages are slitting our family members' throats?

CHAPTER SEVEN

A RAID SCENARIO - SECOND-GUESSING THOSE AT THE TIP OF THE SPEAR

WITH
JOHN TAYLOR

Certain government leaders went into a mild panic over the 2016 publication of Sean Naylor's new book *Relentless Strike: The Secret History of Joint Special Operations Command*. Since it would be inappropriate to comment on the veracity of anything Naylor has written about that command, our focus is on one seemingly innocuous and completely unclassified portion of his book. The following paragraphs are within our particular skill sets – the laws and tactical realities surrounding deadly force encounters – and it bears commenting upon.

> *When "clearing" a building—i.e., moving through it and eliminating any threats— Rangers flowed through the structure like water, scanning each room in a synchronized choreography that was the result of hundreds of repetitions*

in training and combat. Only if they found any military-age men would the Rangers pause momentarily to leave a couple of soldiers to watch that room as the others continued through the building. It was not unusual for the Rangers to clear a compound in less than twenty seconds. The living room opened to a hallway that led to a corridor with several bedrooms. In the first, the squad leader and a young Ranger found a man and woman sleeping on mats. Using memorized Arabic, the squad leader, who was a battle-hardened staff sergeant, and the other soldier— a twenty-one-year-old specialist armed with a light machine gun called a squad automatic weapon— told the couple to put their hands up. Neither did. The two Rangers repeated the order, as their colleagues checked the corridor's other rooms, finding two women and several children. But instead of putting his hands above his head as ordered, the man in the first room made as if to reach inside his robe. The squad leader's finger tightened on the trigger of his M4. He had less than a second to make a life-or-death decision.

The squad leader made his decision. He pulled the trigger, shooting the man in the head. Realizing what his squad leader was going to do, the specialist did the same, firing a burst with his squad automatic weapon. Their reaction "was aggressive," said another Ranger later, with studied understatement. If it turned out that the man was unarmed, there would be consequences. The squad leader reported the room "clear and secure" and left the specialist to guard the woman. Above them, the sniper team leader shot and killed the second gunman on the roof. But as soon as the squad leader had left the room, the woman dove *toward the body of her husband. Again the specialist had to make a split-second decision. Again his instinct told him to pull the trigger. He fired a short burst and the woman's head split apart. With the squad momentarily distracted by the firing, a figure darted from the last room left to be cleared and ran up the stairs clutching a pistol. He burst out of the cupola, only for the sniper team leader to put two bullets in his head. The gunman's lifeless body toppled back through the cupola and fell to the ground floor, crashing into a Ranger, the impact tearing the latter's night vision goggles from his face. Abu Khalaf was dead. The Rangers had been in the house for less than thirty seconds.*

With the house finally cleared and all the adult males killed, the Rangers began the exploitation phase of the mission. An examination of the dead man in the first bedroom revealed a suicide vest. Had the two Rangers not fired when they did, they and perhaps several of their comrades would have died. Honed in nine combat deployments, the squad leader's instinct had saved numerous lives, as had the specialist's decision to open fire on the woman. She was the first woman that platoon had shot in about 200 missions. That there had been shooting at all was unusual. Only about 10 percent of the platoon's missions involved gunfights.[1]

Naylor has unwittingly hit upon a persistent and dangerous misunderstanding concerning the use of force that exists among many members of the press, civilian leaders, civilian attorneys, military commanders, and military judge advocates, to wit: a soldier or police officer who uses deadly force must always be right or correct in his decision to use deadly force for that use of deadly force to be lawful. This is absolutely false. Unfortunately, far too many military personnel are sitting in Leavenworth cells due to ignorance about this issue. Let's quickly examine why we say this:

1 So, what if the suspect was unarmed and there was no suicide vest, would the young Ranger's actions have been any less lawful? Absolutely not. Constitutional law in the United States does not require FBI agents and other law enforcement officers to be right; only reasonable. That same deference must be given to a company of Rangers in Afghanistan, operating under use of force rules that are clearly not intended to be *more* restrictive than those governing a law enforcement officer operating in a Constitutional Fourth Amendment environment in the United States.

2 Does the fact that the second suspect was a woman have any bearing on the lawfulness of the shoot? Absolutely not. A fourteen-year-old girl with an AK-47 can kill you just as dead as a 24-year-old committed Jihadist. Besides, wasn't the Obama Administration itching to get females into direct combat units? They can't have it both ways.

3 Does the fact that 90 percent of the capture missions did not require the use of deadly force in any way impact the lawfulness of the two Rangers' use of force? Not in the least. Police officers are assaulted at least 60,000 times a year, 15,500 times with a dangerous and deadly weapon, and they only kill approximately 600 suspects a year.[2] One cannot use metrics to assess the reasonableness of

shooting in self-defense. Each case must be judged according to its own merits.

So, the answer to all three questions, above, is an unequivocal "NO!" But, just as in domestic law enforcement shootings, too many commentators make a big deal about an irrelevancy that the now dead suspect was unarmed. Clucking their figurative tongues, they write as if that single issue is entirely dispositive on the question of whether a shooting by police was lawful. It may be one of many factors in the overall analysis or it may be entirely irrelevant to the ultimate lawfulness of the use of deadly force. It certainly is not the single dispositive factor that the Black Lives Matter crowd asserts. And citizens need to be educated about this because it is critically important both for military personnel and cops today in this increasingly violent insurgency that such Fifth Columnists have started in our Republic.

In as easy a picture as we can paint, people who follow directions of cops or military personnel who are pointing guns at them are *rarely* if ever shot. The sad and frequently repeated situation occurs when a suspect or detainee fails to do what they're repeatedly told to do by lawful authorities and then make a furtive gesture or engage in some other threatening conduct. As a consequence of that refusal and accompanying conduct, they get shot and/or killed. Then, the poor devils that shoot them, merely trying to survive and do their jobs, get prosecuted. And this, in a nutshell, is the source of frustration among cops and soldiers across America and amongst real experts in the use of deadly force:[3] why are some members of the public siding with those here and abroad who disobey lawful authority figures and place themselves at greater risk by their own freely chosen misbehavior and ill conduct?

CHAPTER EIGHT

TOXIC LEADERSHIP AND DANGEROUS RULES OF ENGAGEMENT

As reported by Rowan Scarborough's 2015 *Washington Times* article, "Increase in Battlefield Deaths Linked to Rules of Engagement," the Obama administration's imposition of even more restrictive rules of engagement for our forces in Afghanistan was deeply troubling. Of particular concern is the fact that America has been at war for over fifteen years and our country's senior civilian and military leaders are still woefully, perhaps even willfully, ignorant of the ethical, tactical, and legal realities concerning the use of force in self-defense. Due to their unnecessary insistence that so-called human rights law be fused into the traditional law of war standards, America's warriors will lose the benefit of the doubt in life and death situations. Army Lieutenant Clint Lorance, convicted in 2013 at Fort Bragg for ordering his soldiers to shoot three Afghan suspects on a motorcycle in a Taliban-controlled area of Afghanistan, is only one exemplar of such folly. Captain Roger Hill and his band of brothers in Dog Company 1-506 Infantry was another. Hill's and Lynn Vincent's book *Dog Company* will be a must read for any student of military history and the inherent threat of Islam.

On the campaign trail in 2008, Barack Obama promised to get the United States out of Afghanistan. Eight years later, our forces were still there, targets of the Taliban and "inside the wire" killings by our putative allies. When administration and even senior military leaders are asked why we are still in Afghanistan, they all mumble and mutter for ten or fifteen minutes, but never answer the question. In World War II, had any senior leader or Private been asked a similar question, they could have answered in a sentence, "To defeat Nazi Germany and Imperial Japan in order to save the world from tyranny." If we have now been at war for thrice as long as World War II, ought we not know why we are fighting? If the current crop of leaders and lawyers were running the show back in 1944, the entire E Company, 506th Parachute Infantry Regiment of *Band of Brothers* fame would have been court-martialed. Moreover, we would now all be speaking German.

Since the likelihood of getting a straight answer from most of the senior military leaders that have survived Obama's purge is minimal; We, The People should at a minimum demand that our warriors be given *at least* the protection of law given FBI agents and other law enforcement officers here on the streets of America. That standard, that special agents will not be judged in the clear vision of 20/20 hindsight, but rather on how a reasonable person would react under situations that are tense, uncertain and rapidly evolving, is based on hundreds of years of constitutional and common law standards. It was echoed by Louis Freeh when he was FBI director as a sign that his agents would have the political backing of the Agency should they have to use deadly force in the line of duty. Instead of providing such clear and courageous leadership, America's senior political and military managers (they do not deserve to be called leaders) have ratcheted down on artificial and tactically impractical rules in a specious attempt to prevent casualties of war.

Our policy makers have decided to employ a blunt instrument, the military, to perform precision surgery in Afghanistan. They should not be surprised when trauma results to the patient. And they ought not to hold those at the tip of the spear responsible. We haven't seen any politician or general officer charged criminally for collateral damage deaths caused when they drop a JDAAM or fire a Hellfire from a Predator. Why are soldiers like Lieutenant Lorance charged with murder when they make split-second decisions at the tip of the spear in Afghanistan? The answer is two-fold. First, there are rampant misunderstandings of the law of war throughout our forces. Secondly, cowardice and toxic leadership at our republic's highest levels.

The law of war does not require such distinction in targeting at either the operations or tactical level. It is only when policy makers and their lawyers improperly try to infuse human rights law onto the battlefield that these matters become an affront to the International Committee of the Red Cross (ICRC). In turn, because there some that believe that the United States should follow every whim of the ICRC, this has created an unnecessary bogie monster that looms over every level of command.

The enemy has become quite adept at using this tactic of "lawfare" to make us chase our own tails and be much less combat effective. Too many commanders are now so afraid to use force when our troops are under attack (just ask Medal of Honor recipient Dakota Myers at the Battle of Ganjgal) that they will sit on their hands rather than order artillery fire in response. They do not want to risk their next promotion by making a decision that might be questioned after the fact. The Obama administration's agreement to Afghan rules that further restrict both the general in the tactical operation center and the warriors in the field only exacerbated this pitiful state.

Misunderstanding of such complex and obtuse rules breeds unnecessary confusion and hesitation among the force. This confusion will result not only in unnecessary risks to our forces but also in our young warriors' persistent exposure to criminal liability for the perceived crime of killing the enemy. More disturbingly, the Administration has mistakenly equated the value of American lives with those of the enemy. Again, we should take to heart Winston Churchill's quote, "I refuse to remain neutral between the fire and the fire brigade."

In addition to needlessly exposing our warriors to threats in today's battlefields, this mindset of warfare by lawfare has ominous implications for the future as well. We have created toxic leaders who wring their hands over every silly edict from above: in essence, more concerned about their careers than their subordinates' lives or killing bad guys. Former Chief of Staff of the Army, General Eric K. Shinseki, once observed, "You must love those that you lead before you can be an effective leader." To love one's subordinates requires humility. That virtue is the most important, yet seemingly most difficult to obtain, element of leadership. It is the lack of humility that underscores the recent missteps by some of our senior flag officers, to include Generals David Petreaus and Kip Ward.

While instructing at the US Army War College, I had the privilege of spending many hours with some of America's finest warrior-leaders. Many had just finished either their battalion or brigade command tours in combat theaters. During more candid discussions with these mostly humble men and women, a disturbing pattern of stories that kept surfacing concerning our senior leaders. Two brief exemplars to illustrate their concern.

An Army Major General, then Commander of the 3rd Infantry Division, on the rare occasion that he would leave the safe confines of his command post (CP), would exit his transport helicopter and then theatrically stand in a crucifix-like pose. Arms outstretched, he would expect his junior enlisted aides to dress him with his pistol belt, body armor and web gear. He would then strut about abusing and upbraiding junior officers in front of their subordinates before quickly boarding the helicopter for the ride back to the safety of the CP. At the twice-daily battle update briefs, this commander would demand that all his staff officers sing "The Dogface Soldier," 3rd Infantry Division's official song. Before the briefing began, in a truly Stanley Kubrickesque fashion, the Division Chief of Staff, a senior Army Colonel, would walk around the large conference table making sure that each staff member was singing with equal enthusiasm. The briefings quickly devolved into one-way screaming sessions where the commander would embarrass and yell at subordinates who attempted to offer a differing viewpoint on a plan or mission. Sadly, this is the same 3rd Infantry Division once commanded by Lucian Truscott in World War II or, more recently, by David Grange: two officers who would go to the mat for subordinates and encourage positive dissent in operational planning.

An Air Force General, then in command of one of the United States' unified commands, the pinnacle of uniformed command, would also routinely abuse subordinates in public and encourage sycophancy. He would demand every creature comfort for himself and his family. At his headquarters building, he would block the use of the elevators by subordinates in the off chance he may use it. Full bird colonels would literally stand guard to prevent other personnel from boarding the elevator because "the General may be coming." Besides the jaw-dropping waste of resources this represents (one would hope that colonels would have more important duties at their $155,000–a-year salary than to hold elevators for egomaniacal generals) the sad fact is that most officers in this headquarters aspired for general officer rank not for the privilege of leading others but rather for the silly perquisites they believed the position deserved. This same four-star commander's wife, during one of the myriad overseas trips she took with her husband at taxpayer expense, brought home twenty-nine pairs of Jimmy Choo shoes (for those not in the know about fashion shoes – I had to ask my wife what "Jimmy Choos" were - may be surprised to learn that each pair costs, on average, about $2,000!), "gifts" from some foreign potentate seeking favor with the United States.

Such accounts raise many questions of how, institutionally, America's military breeds such abominations of leadership. One could blame of culture of toadyism that accepts, nay *expects*, gross entitlements for senior officers. Or one might try to rationalize such excesses by saying that a general officer should not or cannot take time from his already busy schedule to endure such egalitarian indignities as sharing an elevator with a subordinate. The latter is true to a point; that is why generals in command positions have aides to pack their bags, arrange their calendars, and make their airline reservations. However, this privilege has extended to an absurd sense of entitlement where leaders *expect* doors to be held open for them.

Lack of humility is at the center of these accounts and is the root of what we now call "toxic leadership." Such a seemingly blinding flash of the obvious, however, must be seen in relation to how all the virtues are combined in truly great leaders. Ethicist Alexander Havard, author of *Virtuous Leadership*, describes how great leaders must overlay the four basic virtues of courage, competency, self-control and justice with two supernumerary virtues of magnanimity and humility.

While magnanimity, the endeavor to compel greatness in self, others and mission, is important and often overlooked, humility is what is too often lacking in many of our senior military leaders. It is humility that allows great leaders to be servant leaders. The ability to figuratively wash the feet of others is seen in leaders who truly care about the welfare of their subordinates. A humble leader would never send a subordinate on a task without purpose; would never eat, sleep or travel in greater comfort than others in their command; and, would never come to expect undue privileges or tolerate boot licking by subordinates.

While, in the end, the etiology of toxic leadership is probably a complex web of sociological and psychological ills, two possible solutions would be fairly easily and inexpensively implemented. First, the institution must instill a deeper understanding of the importance of humility in its educational structure. Second, the military should adopt a true 360-degree rating system that includes peers and subordinates.

Educationally, at the very minimum, intermediate and senior service schools for officers and enlisted personnel should adopt a curriculum that includes many more hours studying and reflecting upon the nature of virtuous leadership. Socially and historically, such study is more likely to produce leaders like Generals Shinseki, Robert E. Lee, Truscott and Marshall. History is full of virtuous leaders, and the study of their humble nature is worth the journey. Humility, too, is often discovered when studying the history of heroic action.

In *Forgotten Voices*, Roderick Bailey's collection of stories about recipients of the Victoria Cross (the United Kingdom's equivalent of the Medal of Honor) it is observed that "striking is the modesty, understatement and self-deprecation that runs through the accounts of those awarded the Victoria Cross. The words of Patrick Porteous, for example, a commando officer who earned the medal in the 1942 raid on the French port of Dieppe, are made no less revealing by the fact that it is left to other soldiers to draw attention to his courage." Such humility cannot be recounted too often or its importance stressed too much. Leaders that work in a system that constantly encourages humility would be far less susceptible to falling into the crippling sense of entitlement that is now so rampant.

Secondly, a true 360-degree officer evaluation system would infuse a promotion system with the opinions of not only superiors, but also peers and subordinates. Not only would this help weed out toxic leaders who often hide their defects from superiors, but it would also help break the chain of whereby promotion board members pick mirror images of themselves. In the Army, for instance, the current system produced a lineage of officers tracing their roots to Wesley Clark's "Bosnian Mafia" or, more recently, to those swallowing the Counter-Insurgency (COIN) KoolAid of David Petraeus. Such a system might be good if a George Marshall "self selects," but not so good if a leader lacking the virtue of humility chooses like-minded subordinates for promotion. True leaders have nothing to fear if the opinions of their peers and subordinates are considered for rating and promotional purposes.

Seniors wishing to unduly influence the selection of their replacements, however, will strongly balk at this recommendation. Good men have nothing to hide or fear from such a system. A fair servant leader, even while demanding excellence, is respected by his peers and most revered by his subordinates. Historical examples include Jim Gavin, who commanded the 82nd Airborne Division during most of WWII and, more recently, Marine General James Mattis (President Trump's Secretary of Defense), Commander of US Central Command, who formerly led the 1st Marine Division during the Invasion of Iraq in 2003.

In the end, humility can be taught and rewarded. Our military should find and encourage ways to do so as its young warriors and our country deserve no less. Good men have nothing to hide or fear from these changes. A revamping of the rating systems to include input from peers and subordinates would directly help weed out many toxic leaders with a sense of entitlement. The pushback from the uniformed services would be tremendous, as those in leadership positions feel that they are entitled to select their successors. The problem is that they are often blinded by their own experiences (sorely limited availability heuristics) and continue to select subordinates that follow a set career path. It would require intervention from Congress or the civilian leadership within DoD to force this change. The changes to the services' educational system would be easier, but would still require a mandate from the top to ensure the quality and efficacy of such a program. The American military enjoys a tremendous respect and admiration from its citizens. However, if it does not take serious steps to shore up its culture, it risks losing that respect. More importantly, it risks losing its ability to effectively defend the Republic against a determined peer-competitor enemy like China's PLA.

CHAPTER NINE

PAYING DANE GELD

As the author is a Delawarean, I was dismayed in 2016 to read that morning's headlines that announced that Senator Chris Coons (D-DE) flip-flopped and supported Barack Obama's insane nuclear pact with Iran. This deal not only ensured a fanatical state supporter of terrorism will be nuclear-armed, but also that the state of Israel will face an existential threat. This is not a negative fantasy or hyperbole; rather, it is the stated goal of Iran's political and theocratic leadership, as it has been since 1979 when the Ayatollah Khomeini displaced the Shah of Iran during another weak Democratic presidency, that of Jimmy Carter. We wonder what pressure or backroom deal was excerpted upon Coons, but he and others in the Senate would be well served to read Rudyard Kipling's poem *Dane Geld*, the first and last stanzas which read:

> *It is always a temptation to an armed and agile nation*
> *To call upon a neighbour and to say: --*
> *"We invaded you last night--we are quite prepared to fight,*
> *Unless you pay us cash to go away."*
> *So when you are requested to pay up or be molested,*
> *You will find it better policy to say: --*

"We never pay any-one Dane-geld,
No matter how trifling the cost;
For the end of that game is oppression and shame,
And the nation that pays it is lost!"

Not coincidentally, Great Britain's 22nd Special Air Service (SAS) Regiment presented the US Army's 1st Special Forces Operations Detachment- Delta (Delta Force) a bronzed relief of this poem, and it is prominently displayed in that unit's headquarters. Thankfully, President Obama didn't give it back to England as he did with that country's magnanimous gift of a bust of Winston Churchill. One of Donald Trump's first official acts as President was to restore Churchill's bust to the Oval Office.

Americans have lost their sense of self-reliance and, in turn, believe that "the government" will be there to "rescue" them in the face of any threat. Hollywood would have us believe that SEAL Team 6 or *24*'s Jack Bauer will always come the rescue. This is a blindly ignorant and cowardly way to live. We should never have forgotten how important it is to teach our sons to "ride, shoot straight and tell the truth." For if we don't, as Senator Coons and Barack Obama have demonstrated with Iran, we will always pay the *Dane Geld*. And, on the specific occasion of paying ransom for the release of our sailors captured in the Persian Gulf, such *Geld* was to the tune of at least $400 million, all from the coffers of the United States Treasury without Congressional authorization or appropriation in violation of our Constitution.[1]

Logically and prayerfully, this single issue alone ought to have unraveled the unholy alliance American Jewry has had with the Progressive Party ever since they wrongfully perceived

FDR as their savior from the National Socialists in Germany. In fact, Progressives, especially President Obama, are closet anti-Semites who see government as god instead of Yahweh. Many erstwhile Jewish Democrats are beginning to see that true Liberalism, believing in the rights and power of the individual over that of that of the sovereign, is not the spirit of their current political party.

Again, Scripture speaks of the difference between those that are woefully ignorant and those that are willfully ignorant. The former are educable while the latter damnable. By his act, Coons squarely places himself in the latter camp. For America's sake and Israel's survival, we should all offer up a prayer that no more politicians like Chris Coons imprudently turn their backs on what is right here. Iran must not obtain nuclear weapons. At any cost![2]

CHAPTER TEN

TEXAS, ISLAM, AND AMERICA - IDENTIFYING AND TARGETING THE THREAT

An armed attack near Dallas, Texas in May 2015 by two radical Islamic Muj gunmen inspired me to write these observations. The sponsors of the underlying event, a contest to draw artwork depicting the Prophet Mohammed, are akin to Winston Churchill, who had the courage in the 1930s to warn against the existential threat posed by the military buildup of Nazi Germany and Imperial Japan. Today, radical Islam poses an existential threat to what collectively we know as the West. Any voice that warns of this threat should be trumpeted not silenced by political correctness.

As Christians, we have had a lifetime of being offended by Western artists who denigrate Christ and the crucifix, the most notorious example being the work *Piss Christ* that was comprised of an upside-down crucifix suspended in a translucent cylinder of urine. We were deeply offended when radical homosexuals threw semen-filled condoms on the altars of our church. Yet, never have my fellow Christians or I demanded that such acts of free speech be suspended. And, certainly we have never endorsed killing or stoning of those holding differing religious or political views. In the twenty-first century, only radical Islam appears to be incompatible with a constitutional republican form of governance, free speech, and a free lifestyle.

Many in the progressive media and body politic are now blaming Geert Wilders, Pamela Geller, and the Dallas event's organizers for inciting this act of violence. This is both cowardly and illogical. Those opposed to the event would have no problem shutting down a Christmas pageant in the name of the First Amendment, yet see no irony in endorsing inclusion of Sharia law into our system of justice. This mentality is on par with Chamberlain's "peace in our time" myopia during Hitler's era. Instead of placating radical Islamists (or, as the Southern Poverty Law Center has done, simply reverting to the ad hominem by calling those that highlight its dangers "racists" or "hate groups"), we ought to hunt them down root and branch for incarceration, deportation or, as necessary, lethal targeting.

America is a tolerant nation that openly welcomes all races, creeds, and nationalities. All we ask in return is hard work and obeisance to our constitutional principles and rule of law. Some Muslims seem to get this concept and we should welcome them into our society. Those who cannot abide by this fair and just exchange need to be identified and excluded with extreme prejudice. I would rather kill them overseas, where they are less of a threat to my family, friends and neighbors; but Texas will do.

CHAPTER ELEVEN

TSA: WORKFARE FOR THOSE WHO WANT TO HASSLE FELLOW AMERICANS

I am writing on a subject that most are no doubt painfully aware; yet, something must be done to disassemble this bureaucratic monster that has made flying on commercial aircraft in America painful at best. When I took my first flight from Baltimore's Friendship Airport to Louisville in 1968, it was an exciting, genteel, and totally pleasant experience. My parents – as did anyone, accompanied me right to the gate. That was in 1968. I never envisioned that forty-eight years later our republic would treat most citizens taking to the friendly skies as criminal suspects.

Recently, for instance, while flying round-trip from Atlanta to Philadelphia, I was subjected to the most rude and surly behavior by TSA "agents." As an honorably discharged and retired three-tour combat veteran and law enforcement officer, I have possessed a TS-SCI clearance for most of my adult life. Despite this, and for no apparent reason, I was singled out for special treatment by a pack of borderline illiterate TSA employees. As my wife was whisked through, they made me wait as dozens of other travelers cruised by. Then, even after going through the L3 Com body scanner, they felt I necessary to frisk me like a criminal perpetrator in front of three hundred fellow travelers. When I asked why, I received no reply other than a surly, "Sir, stand over there!" In addition to my embarrassment, it angers me that we have devolved to the point that we have to quietly eat this gross infringement on our personal liberties. God forbid one pushes back against this insanity.

A few months later, I was flying from Dallas to Philadelphia. The agent handling our checked bags (with firearms) was delightfully professional and pleasant. Unfortunately, this professionalism turned to shit as I went through the screening process at the gate. *After* telling the agents in the screening area that, (1), I was a Stage IV cancer survivor, and (2) I had an artificial hip, an agent singled me out for special treatment. "Stand over there!" No please, Sir, or thanks, just belligerent grunts rudely directed at me.

I again came within a hair's breadth of knocking his teeth down his throat, but I kept my cool, knowing that a physical altercation and my arrest would ensue. My law enforcement colleague who witnessed this event was outraged. He wanted to seek out the TSA supervisor. I told him, "Not worth the hassle, because they don't give a crap either. As an older white, Christian male, I am an easy, safe target for them."

Also, I do not buy the line, "Well, at least it makes us safe." As someone who has worked directly with some of our nation's most sensitive counter-terror intelligence units, that dog doesn't hunt with me. First, the enemy has already used that tactic, technique, and procedure (TTP); the cow's out of the barn, so why keep shutting the barn door on our fellow law-abiding citizens? Secondly, I think I have more than proven that I am one of the *good* guys. What more ought I do to show my fidelity and loyalty to our flag and republic? By the way, I already have TSA Precheck; apparently, all for naught.

TSA has made flying so freaking miserable that I will no longer fly to any destination where I can drive a car to in ten hours or less. But, that still leaves most Americans vulnerable to the retributive, snotty TSA agents who screw with people because they can. I also do not buy that line of deflecting responsibility that goes, "They are just doing their job!" As Paul Newman stated so eloquently in the movie *Cool Hand Luke*, "Calling it your job, Boss, don't make it right!"

There are better, more efficient ways to cull out potential terrorists from the herd. It is a clue to all but the deliberately blind that radical Islamists perpetrate the vast majority of terror attacks. It is not the vast majority of my fellow travelers. Despite this blinding flash of the obvious, why does TSA irrationally and mindlessly mess with law-abiding folks? It appears the sole answer is, "Because they can." It is getting nigh on time to try better ways lest otherwise lawful Americans start pushing back in manners not envisioned by bureaucrats in Washington or the bullies at the gate.

One option simply might be to hire quality intelligence analysts[1] using facial recognition software, much as the Israelis do on *El Al*, to focus on those most likely to commit an act of terror. TSA ought not be a workfare program for imbeciles simply because their leadership lacks the *intelligence* and *integrity* to demand good hires and the ability to target probable suspects.

One might easily dismiss this as the mere rants of an old soldier and cop; but, trust me, I am not alone in my feelings that our government is becoming seriously disconnected from

We, the People it ought to serve. If such problems are not solved peaceably through the legislative process, Congress reining in an out-of-control executive branch, good folks will reach a point where they will start pushing back. I do not want this to happen, but the undercurrent of frustration amongst many of my fellow law enforcement officers and combat veterans may present unintended consequences to an overreaching, all-powerful government. TSA is just the most visible example of which I speak. It is better to stop the harassment now before people like me start pushing back.

If we can no longer go out to the gate to meet loved ones returning from a trip, just as I did back in the 60s, then the terrorists have won. Along with my many colleagues who were wounded or died in combat tours in Iraq, Afghanistan, and other really crappy places, I now ask, "Why did we fight, if this is how we are to be treated by fellow Americans?" By reacting to the terror strikes by treating citizens as suspects, the nation shows cowardice, ineptitude, and rudeness. Hiding behind the skirts of the TSA, Americans are no safer and a whole lot less free. This last point is what worries me most. We are beginning to fear Islamists less than sectors of our own republic.

CHAPTER TWELVE

MATHEW GOLSTEYN AND ROGER HILL - HEROES BY ANY OTHER NAME

WITH
JOHN TAYLOR

The cases of US Army Major Mathew L. Golsteyn and Captain Roger Hill might be a microcosm of much of what is wrong with how the United States has conducted warfare since the end of World War II. Golsteyn, a decorated Special Forces officer (or "Green Beret" in civilian parlance) was nominated to receive the Distinguished Service Cross (DSC), our nation's second-highest award for valor, when he was subsequently investigated, but not prosecuted, for alleged war crimes violations. In short, he supposedly admitted in a CIA pre-employment polygraph that he had executed a Taliban bomb maker responsible for killing and maiming US military personnel in Afghanistan. Captain Roger Hill, commander of Dog Company 1-506 Infantry, 101st Airborne Division did nothing more than coerce by ruse three Taliban informers to admit their treachery in causing the deaths and injuries to Hill's men in 2008. Hill's experiences are beautifully recounted in *Dog Company: A True Story of Enemy Spies, Battlefield Courage,* *and Soldiers on Trial in Afghanista*n by Lynn Vincent and Roger Hill. The book will make you cry in anger. Hill's rifle company of less than one hundred men had to control a battle space the size of Connecticut in an Afghan province littered with Taliban. Through classified sources and a Special Forces team leader collocated with Hill's unit, he discovered that thirteen spies, supposedly vetted by NATO, were working on his base camp. One of the spies was Hill's own interpreter. All were feeding critical information to the Taliban, often causing death and injury to Hill's men. He was not allowed to use the classified information to detain these traitors beyond 96 hours. In fact, according to NATO rules in place, he was supposed to release them and give them $200 as well! So, Roger Hill used inventive interrogation methods that amounted to nothing more than a ruse to gain confessions. But, in this era of inanely restrictive legal oversight, some shave tail lieutenant reported his actions to higher headquarters as a "war crime." What happened next is truly Orwellian in nature and will make any patriotic American's blood boil. Buy and read *Dog Company* in order to gain a meaningful understanding of how corrupt and weak our military leaders have become.

In Goldsteyn's case, without the benefit of a trial or hearing, the Army has ignominiously and publicly stripped him of all his prior awards, including the Silver Star, the nation's third-highest decoration for valor in combat, his Special Forces (SF) tab, and his reputation. This is not how the American system of justice is supposed to work. Has not the Army leadership heard of the presumption of innocence or the burden of proof? One does not eviscerate a confirmed hero based on rumor, innuendo and probably unlawfully leaked unsworn answers to a pre-employment polygraph. Such statements are inadmissible in American courtrooms for a reason: they are notoriously inaccurate and often result in false confessions.

But, the Army has publicly claimed they have probable cause to support the underlying charges of murder. Probable cause is nearly the lowest form of proof available in the legal system. All it means is "a reasonable amount of suspicion, supported by circumstances sufficiently strong to justify a prudent and cautious person's belief that certain facts are probably true." It is less than a preponderance of the evidence, which is what is required to prevail in a civil law suit. It is much lower than the level of proof required for conviction in a criminal proceeding, which is beyond a reasonable doubt.

Given the extremely serious nature of the allegation, the Army should prefer charges against Golsteyn pursuant to the Uniform Code of Military Justice and let this heroic officer defend himself against the charges in a criminal court. If he is found not guilty, he should be afforded all the honors and courtesies to which he is entitled: to include restoration of his Silver Star and, possibly, the DSC. We afford the same privilege to drug dealers. Ought not our nation afford the same due process to a warrior?

But this is the glaring issue. The more subtle issues are legion:

First, procedurally, how did the Army obtain Major Golsteyn's confidential polygraph answers? Pre-employment polygraph statements made to the nations' leading spy agency are presumably confidential in nature. This is especially true for the so-called lifestyle background polygraph examinations, where prospective employees are asked intimate and personal questions. The end result of failing one of these subjective inquisitions is that one is not offered a position with the agency.

Such backdoor shenanigans call into question the veracity and integrity of the very program that is supposedly conducting security clearance investigations. Why would any candidate for the CIA's operational ground elements ever voluntarily subject themselves to a lifestyle polygraph examination if the answers, criminal or embarrassing, are likely to leak to the public in the sieve that is Washington, DC, and be made available, again probably unlawfully, to a current employer or the media?

Second, legally, a bald confession unsupported by any corroborating evidence is insufficient to support a criminal complaint. If it really happened and the Army has the evidence to support that claim, then charge him and conduct a General Court-Martial. If it involves classified activities, there are well-established procedures for conducting a closed trial. Instead, the Army engages in underhanded character assassination, what in civilian terms is generally referred to as slander, by leaking probably classified and certainly privileged information to the public to justify its actions.

And what is the wrongdoing that Major Golsteyn is accused of? He allegedly murdered an unarmed illegal combatant. This is one of the worst allegations one can make against a soldier during time of war. And for that transgression the Army has decided that an adverse administrative discharge is the appropriate punishment? They can't be serious. To put this in terms many Americans would understand, this is the equivalent of a police officer gunning down an unarmed suspect in police custody and then being fired for it, with no other punishment. This is certainly an absurd result for a nation that purportedly values and upholds the rule of law. It is the equivalent of tolerating war crimes by its military forces. If the Army *truly* believes this happened then they are obligated to prosecute this officer to the fullest extent of the law, come what may. Otherwise this childish and petulant campaign of character assassination, and their wholly inadequate "firing" of that officer, treats a vile war crime as an act of workplace misconduct. This cannot be allowed to stand. If the Army does not have proof, then it didn't happen, regardless of what their unseemly campaign of mud slinging would have the public believe about what Major Golsteyn purportedly told a polygrapher at the CIA (hardly the paradigm of virtue itself).

Third, it appears that all the Army's subsequent investigation uncovered was the possibility that Golsteyn had drank a shot of whisky while toasting fallen comrades with his fellow warriors. This would be in violation of General Order #1, a ridiculously restrictive proscription on alcohol consumption that the US military has had in place for every operation in the region since Desert Storm, for fear of insulting our Muslim allies. One has to marvel at one lieutenant colonel interviewed who was upset because, horrors of horrors, this Special Forces team leader drank a shot of booze with his fellow warriors. In addition to being pure PC pandering to our putative Muslim hosts, most of our allies, including Great Britain and France, do not similarly restrict their troops. Perversely, this is the same Army that decades earlier used to sling-load pallets of beer into fire bases in Vietnam. Who would have thought that alcohol would become taboo for soldiers risking their lives for their country in a mere thirty years" This holier than thou, "My God, he drank alcohol in theater" attitude is laughable. Most men, including us, did not hesitate to share a toast of victory with our comrades.

Fourth, the Army should not revoke valor awards that a soldier clearly earned for actions that had nothing to do with the subsequent allegations of misconduct. Major Golsteyn also earned his Special Forces tab by successfully completing the grueling qualification course. Why take that from him too? Absent some proof – not mere suspicion or innuendo– this piecemeal and backhanded approach to justice reeks of smoky backroom Chicago politics and teenaged petulance.

Finally, at a visceral level, like Roger Hill's, Golsteyn's alleged misconduct made sense. He did not kill a farmer or peasant or other innocent. He killed a known Muj bomb maker. So, the notion that he murdered a protected person is morally debatable. One might reasonably believe that the CIA position for which he was being polygraphed did not involve treating such vermin with politeness. These same Taliban and other Islamists groups routinely murder civilians and commit gross violations of the law of armed conflict. How many of these terrorists have we prosecuted for actual war crimes? Hint: it rhymes with Nero and begins with a *Z*.

Instead, we are essentially being told, "Trust us, we are the Army." This smells of Army "third file" nonsense. One's "third file" is akin to "the Vault" described by Burt Lancaster's character in *Go Tell the Spartans,* a movie about US Army military advisors during the early part of the Vietnam War in 1964. In that film, Lancaster's character is asked why he hasn't been promoted in light of his distinguished combat record. He says that his name is in "the Vault" for past indiscretions. The Army is notorious for making personnel decisions based on sycophancy, rumor, and "third files." It seems Major Mathew Golsteyn's name has been added to the Vault.

In constitutional republics, we should not have "Vaults" or "third files." In unchecked bureaucracies, however, they do. The handling of this matter indicates that the bureaucrats have indeed won: at least for now. It will take a shooting war on the scale of WWII to rid our military of mediocre leaders steeped in timidity and replace them with steely-eyed killers like Mathew Golsteyn. We only hope America and Western Civilization can survive that long before either Mohammedanism or Globalism gobbles it up. Hopefully, appointing General James Mattis as Secretary of Defense ought to get the Department of Defense back on track.

CHAPTER THIRTEEN

THE UGLY TRUTH BEHIND BATTLEFIELD MURDER CHARGES

America has been at war for fifteen years, yet many of our military's leaders are still woefully ignorant of the ethical, tactical, and legal realities concerning the use of force in self-defense. Moreover, due to their unnecessary infusion of human rights law into the traditional law of war standards based on humanitarian law, they become incapable of providing the benefit of doubt to the good guys: America's warriors. Lieutenant Clint Lorance, convicted at Fort Bragg for ordering his soldiers to shoot three Afghan men on a motorcycle in a Taliban-controlled area of Afghanistan, is a clear victim of such folly.

In 2007, the author testified in the defense of Marine Lance Corporal Justin Sharratt, one of the Marines court-martialed for their use of force in Haditha, Iraq on November 19, 2005. One of the prime motivations for my deciding to testify was to ensure the correct legal standard was used to judge the reasonableness of the force Sharratt used. The Supreme Court does not even allow law enforcement officers to be personally liable in a civil case unless no reasonable officer would have used force in the same manner. In the seminal case of *Graham v. Connor,* the Court said that "such reasonableness must be judged from the perspective of a reasonable officer on the scene, rather than with the 20/20 vision of hindsight, the calculus of reasonableness must embody allowance for the fact that police officers are often forced to make split-second judgments about the amount of force that is necessary in a particular situation in circumstances that are tense, uncertain, and rapidly evolving."

The Supreme Court wrote such permissive language because it recognizes the tactical dynamics of such encounters require the greatest latitude be given to an officer acting in the line of duty. It is axiomatic that if such legal protections are given cops stateside, then, at a minimum, Soldiers in a combat zone should be afforded the same. Based on recurring ill-focused investigations, prosecutions and restrictive rules of engagement, it is apparent that this is not happening.

The second prong of my complaint here is based on policy rather than law. There has been a systemic winnowing of steely-eyed killers from our military's senior leader ranks. In their place are effete politicians with Harvard Kennedy School of Government-like credentials; but lacking true, close-in killing experience. Under such leadership, the lives of suspected al Qaeda and Taliban are valued the same as our own young men and women. This misguided approach to fighting a counterinsurgency fails, as Winston Churchill stated, to "decline utterly to be impartial as between the fire brigade and the fire." This raises a serious overarching question, "Why fight?" Again, if the current crop of leaders and lawyers were running the show back in 1944, the entire E Company, 506th Parachute Infantry Regiment of "Band of Brothers" fame would have been court-martialed.

For over fifteen years some of us have endeavored to teach soldiers, sailors, airmen and Marines ways to make better decisions under the stress of CQB. The resultant judgment-based Engagement Training (JET) program uses many lessons learned from law enforcement on how to identify pre-assaultive behaviors and discern between friend and foe. Those so trained are more likely to kill bad guys and less likely to kill noncombatants. The other services have been very receptive to using this training methodology. The Navy even made a professionally produced video about JET. But the Army, with the largest number of deployed troops, remains stubbornly resistant to learning something new. Many of its lawyers refuse to even debate this issue in an open forum, some even try to marginalize by ad hominem those brave enough to question the status quo. If they are afraid of an intellectual knife fight, what good are they in a battle?

Judge Advocates can provide a crucial role in maintaining good order and discipline in the armed forces. Too many are now inserting themselves in roles for which they are inadequately trained. A lawyer should not be making tactical and operational calls as to how and when to target enemies on the field of battle. A one-week operational law course in no manner prepares a young lawyer for understanding the art of war, yet that is exactly what is happening throughout our services. And, sadly, commanders are deferring to the opinions of their lawyers rather than the seasoned warrior at the tip of the spear. Watch the 2015 movie *Eye in the Sky* to gain an appreciation of how truly insane this issue has become.

CHAPTER FOURTEEN

OBAMA'S NATIONAL SECURITY STRATEGY - AN ENEMY WITHIN

On that fateful Friday, that day sacred to government officials desiring to slip bad news to the public with the sincere hope that a weekend of ESPN and Hollywood's latest will distract most citizens, the Obama administration released its new National Security Strategy (NSS). In this document, which is supposed to set forth the priorities and requirements for our national defense, the president placed climate change in the top-tier of the nation's defense priorities. The language of the NSS calls it "an urgent and growing threat." Really? What about Radical Islam, illegals pouring over our borders, a nuclear Iran or China's and Russia's expanding spheres of influence? But the Obama administration even forbade the Pentagon from using the words "Radical Islam" in any of its reports, as if not mentioning them will somehow obviate the threat posed by these devils.

As a retired combat veteran who has personally witnessed strategy being meticulously debated then deployed, I can barely articulate my shock and outrage at this insidious and distracting shibboleth being ranked as a top tier threat to the United States. Radical Islamists are crucifying, shooting, impaling, and burning innocents around the world and here at home. North Korea, Iran, and other unstable nations are rattling their nuclear sabers. Millions of illegal aliens are streaming through our porous borders. Yet, so-called climate change made it to the top of Obama's NSS priorities? This is especially specious in light of the mounting evidence that climate change is pure scientific bunk. Or, as Sherlock Holmes would say, "It is a capital mistake to theorise before one has data. Insensibly one begins to twist facts to suit theories, instead of theories to suit facts." Such is the case with climate change.

Instead of further stating my personal and professional outrage at Obama over his weakening our military strategy (added to his integration of homosexuals and transsexuals into the military force and the helmet fire response to alleged sexual assaults) let me paraphrase two of my colleagues on the NSS debacle. Both are warriors with decades of special operations combat experience:

Ed: "The cowardly silence of the Joint-smoking Chiefs no longer a surprise to me. Climate change. Even to pass this off with a straight face takes a major effort of the will, but of course the current batch of general and flag officers will simply nod solemnly and write command guidance in accordance with the NSS guidance. Then, thousands of field-grade officers will dutifully write the appropriate point papers and PowerPoint slide presentations to educate the military "masses" on the moral imperative of treating Climate Change this with utmost urgency. Online classes on the topic will constitute the next mandatory "training" for our increasingly bewildered and cynical young Soldiers, Sailors, Airmen, and Marines."

Jim: "King Putt just put out his National Security policy. Guess what one of his highest priorities is? Confronting climate change. The Joint Staff idiots actually bought into this. NOT fighting and winning our Nation's wars ... f****ing climate change! That's it, I'm f***ing done. Stick a fork in me. God . . . I cannot get out of this Army quickly enough!"

Jim might have been a little more articulate and less profane, but his passion is well placed. And, the military is losing tens of thousands of experienced warriors such as Ed and Jim.

I will end by again quoting Sherlock Holmes, "A man should keep his little brain-attic stocked with all the furniture that he is likely to use, and the rest he can put away in the lumber-room of his library, where he can get it if he wants it." The United States' brain attic should be concerned with the realistic and existential threats to our country, not the fantasies of Progressivism's lumber-room such as Climate Change. To do otherwise is to place our Republic in mortal danger from the immediate threats of Islam and rogue states like North Korea and potential long-term danger from our peer competitors. It seems that the Trump administration understands this. Time will demonstrate if it can undo the horrific damage of the previous eight years.

BOOK TWO
THE MODERNISTS

CHAPTER FIFTEEN

HARAMBE - WHY IS A GORILLA'S LIFE MORE VALUABLE THAT A HUMAN CHILD'S?

When one mother's son scaled a fence and fell into Harambe the Gorilla's pit at the Cincinnati zoo the week before Memorial Day 2016, she likely had no idea how quickly she would find herself in the national spotlight. As further reported by Kevin Whitson in *Western Journalism*,

"Zoo officials initially felt the brunt of the criticism from those who argued the gorilla's space should not be so easily accessible, and that zoo officials should have tried tranquilizing the gorilla before killing it. But when animal experts such as Jack Hanna defended the zookeepers, critics' attention shifted to the mother, Michelle Gregg, and her parenting skills."

Now let's examine the facts here in light of right reason and all aspects of goodness of our Judeo-Christian ethic that made America a great republic.

First, the four-year-old child's life is worth the life of a million gorillas. Period. This New Age worship of nature and climate change morality has turned the pyramid of God-Man-Animal on its head. Instead of God creating the Earth for Mankind, these Green idiots place man as subservient to Nature. Sadly, Earth Day, the Green alternative to May Day, is becoming the new Christmas, Easter, and Yom Kippur.

Second, a four-year-old child, regardless of the parenting skills of any adult, is apt to wander away and get into mischief. A child of that age will often wandered and get separated from his parents in grocery stores, shopping malls and zoos. That is what the loudspeaker system is for, isn't it? "Little boy with black hair and freckles found near the lion cage. Parents please claim him at the lost and found!" This mother did *nothing* wrong except in the warped world of Progressive helicopter moms who themselves have done much to emasculate America's male children.

Third, the hue and cry over the death of an animal is deeply disturbing in light of the fact that millions of infants have been murdered in these United States since the horrifically anti-Constitutional piece of judicial activism known as *Roe v. Wade*. The Left has successfully made a "woman's right" out of what was once a sin. This twisting of God's commandments has had a terribly deleterious effect on humankind's sympathy for others. Such is very clear in this instance. Instead of feeling, "My gosh, that poor mother," we see and hear the jeers of the crowd screaming to free Barabbas.

Finally, helicopter parenting has also set up a paradigm whereby any child left alone has become prima facie evidence of child abuse. Kids do the darnedest things, and when they do so, it is not evidence of child abuse on the part of the parent. In the summertime not so long ago, six-year-old kids would leave home with friends after breakfast and not return until dinnertime. No adults supervised them as they played tag, baseball or Army. They sure as hell did not need "play dates."

In fact, if dads heard their son was going on a "play date" he would fear the boy was turning into a homosexual!

May God Bless and take care of the mother of this four-year-old. Mercifully, most Americans have the attention span of a gnat. Accordingly, all of this will have been forgotten in the two weeks after the incident, when some more titillating story about Bruce Jenner or another freak show erupted. Until then, she just needed to stay out of the media and harms' way. Prayerfully, she did. But, what about the next time?

CHAPTER SIXTEEN

HOW DO YOU SOLVE A PROBLEM LIKE MILLENNIALS? FOR THEY ARE NOT A FLIBBERTIGIBBET, A WILL-O'-THE WISP, OR A CLOWN!

Talking with a female noncommissioned officer (my wife) and some of her senior military friends, the topics of arose of what has been called the "Millennial Problem."[1] In short, it is an apparent inability of the average twenty-something to cope with adversity and offer selfless service necessary for a victorious military. A great poster illustrating this problem is the following:

We more seasoned officers and noncommissioned officers are partly to blame for this, as we did little to stop helicopter moms and radical Progressives from emasculating our male children or driving from our girls every last vestige of the ability to deal with the vicissitudes of life. Be it not letting them burn piles of leaves in the fall to having play dates instead of just running amok for 8 to 10 hours with the other neighborhood kids, this generation has been coddled like none other in history. We probably were wise not to treat kids as the Spartans did, but we have vectored way too far in the other direction. As

MEN OF COLLEGE AGE LEAVING
THEIR SAFE SPACE

THE GREATEST GENERATION
VS. MILLENNIALS

1944: 18-year-olds stormed beaches,
faced almost certain death & overcame
seemingly insurmountable obstacles.

2016: 18-year-olds need a 'safe space' to
protect them from words.

Politifake.org

a consequence, leaders now have to spend a grossly inordinate amount of time dealing with junior officers and enlisted who are more worried about when they are getting promoted than they are about serving others and the mission.

But, just because our generation bred these pusillanimous, self-centered brats does not mean we must enable them. So, when reading articles or blogs about how we should leverage

Millennial's talents, I sometimes find myself praying for a real shooting war so that the warrior class amongst the whole population will rise to the top of the leadership chain. In lieu of that, it is painful to watch the others pull every EEO, SARC[2], IG lever they can in order to manipulate the system to their facilitate their whims, promotions and "empowerment." (Another word in the progressive lexicon created to defend the indefensible). Not surprisingly, such manipulation of the rules is right out of Saul Alinsky's *Rules for Radicals*. The Progressives have trained their minions well.

The purpose of our military ought to be to close with and destroy our republic's enemies on the seas or fields of battle (Paraphrasing the Army's *Operations Field Manual* from circa 1991, which we used to destroy Saddam's forces in 100 hours in Kuwait). It should never be a workfare program for the otherwise unemployable or a career field for those not interested in helping to kill the enemy. Not every person can be in the infantry, and wars are often won by the support elements; but, every one of those support personnel damned better be able to pick up a rifle when need be and kill the bad guys. It is sickening to watch military leaders tell personnel to run and hide in the event of an Active Shooter event. Criminy, active shooter suspects ought to be frightened of the military, not the other way around! It seems as if the current crop of flag officers who have survived the Obama purges now ask themselves, "What would John Wayne or Ronald Reagan advise?" then do the opposite.

Many young men and women in the Millennial age group possess virtuous character and understand selfless service. In fact, they are magnanimous good citizens. Not surprisingly, many are serving in the fighting branches of our military.

Those seeking the "easy way" typically do not choose these career fields. God has blessed us with them just as he blessed Abraham with Isaac and these words do not apply to them. But they themselves have recognized this whining tendency in many of their erstwhile classmates.

So, absent a cataclysmic Pusan Perimeter-like event, how can the military forge D-Day warriors out of this Charlie Foxtrot? First, some things they have to stop doing: catering to their bitching; jumping through hoops and investigating every little complaint as if it were the Warren Commission; and, lastly, let them fail. This last point is actually meant in the positive, as Machiavelli stated:

> You have to have confidence in your commanders and must give them authority. If they make a mistake out of malice you punish them and if they make a mistake out of ignorance, you actually reward them because you want people to continue to have flexibility and creativity. Desire risk taking in commanders who are not afraid of opportunities.
>
> — *The Discourses On Livy*

Finally, our flag officers have to strenuously push back against their political masters who try and make the military affirm what is otherwise abhorrent, immoral behavior. If little Johnny wants to put on a dress and call himself Jane, that is a choice in life. But, that choice should probably lead to the nuthatch not a military parade in June to affirm such perversions. Bruce Jenner is Bruce Jenner, not Caitlyn and Bradley Manning is Bradley Manning, not Chelsea, Obama's commutation notwithstanding. Again, if a dude cuts off a leg and spray paints his body pink, he is not a flamingo. No matter how fervently he believes it to be so or how many radical Soros funded groups caterwauling that he is, the fact remains that God gave him one *Y* and one *X* chromosome. He is a human male.

All such attempts to deny God and become one's own god should not be celebrated. They should be pitied. Lastly, they need to pay attention to words. On forms, the boxes seeking to know the sex of a person should ask Male or Female? They should not ask one's gender, unless if they are seeking out whether one is masculine or feminine. Words have meaning and we must actively and if need be violently resist those who try to ram gender down our throats.

Some Millennials will simply scoff at this article as the ramblings of an antediluvian. But, those who have lived long enough also realize how much they don't know. So, it may be prudent for them to honestly reflect on their character and life and, as JFK so famously said, "Ask not what your country can do for you, rather what you can do for your country." Hardly the free bill of goods Bernie Sanders, or any other Socialist, appears to be selling.

The republic hangs in the balance. If the virtuous few win the day, America will be in good hands for a time to come. Had the "gimmedat" whiners taken the day and Sanders or Clinton gotten into the White House, many old soldiers would be buying a lot more land, food, water, and ammunition. Because that free shit these two charlatans were promising will run out and we have seen what happens when that occurs. As Prime Minister Lady Margaret Thatcher once presciently observed, "The problem with socialism is that you eventually run out of other people's money.'"

CHAPTER SEVENTEEN

THE DEPARTMENT OF JUSTICE'S UNHOLY VISION OF A NATIONAL POLICE FORCE

WITH
JOHN TAYLOR

The Final Report of the President's Task Force on 21st Century Policing exemplifies the willful mission creep of the Obama administration Department of Justice (DOJ) into matters once reserved for local jurisdictions is so insidious and contrary to the constitutional design of these United States as to be treasonous. DOJ is attempting to make a "one size fits all" police rule book that ignores local mores, culture and rights specifically left to the states under the Tenth Amendment of the Constitution.

One seemingly benign point made in this report is observed in the following quote:

> *How officers define their role will set the tone for the community. As Plato wrote, "In a republic that honors the core of democracy—the greatest amount of power is*

given to those called Guardians. Only those with the most impeccable character are chosen to bear the responsibility of protecting the democracy."

As cogently explained by *Police* magazine's Dave Smith in his article "Warriors or Guardians?"

Plato was no friend of freedom or democracy. His beloved mentor, Socrates, had been executed by the Athenian democracy, and when Plato sought to describe his more perfect world in "The Republic," he portrayed a perfect utopian society run by Guardians: philosopher-kings and their special chosen soldiers who would rule over the simple masses of commoners. That is not a model of policing in a free society, but rather a model for a KGB, Gestapo, or Stasi; indeed, it is for good reason that when Karl Popper wrote "The Open Society and Its Enemies," freedom's first foe was Plato.

Accordingly, these concepts of "national standards" or "DOJ oversight" are simply code words for the Progressives' attempts at controlling true free and classically liberal thought and the right of Americans to freely associate with those of their choosing. The Task Force Commission members, to a person, were all dyed-in-the-wool progressives. This not surprising, considering Obama's track record. Co-chairs of the Commission are **Charles Ramsey** (Former Democratic-appointed Chief of Police of Philadelphia and the District of Columbia) and **Laurie O. Robinson** (former Clinton appointee and current Assistant Attorney General for Obama). Others: **Cedric L. Alexander**, National Second Vice President for the National Organization of Black Law Enforcement

Executives (NOBLE); **Jose Lopez**, (Director, Make the Road New York, an organization that "builds the power of Latino and working class communities to achieve dignity and justice through organizing, policy innovation, transformative education, and survival services."); **Tracey L. Meares**, (Her writings on such issues as crime prevention and community capacity building are concertedly interdisciplinary and reflect a civil society approach to law enforcement that builds upon the interaction between law, culture, social norms, and social organization."); **Brittany N. Packnett,** ("Our children matter deeply, and they should be allowed to live in full dignity, democracy, and freedom, no matter where they live or what they look like."); **Susan Rahr,** ("First Female Sheriff of Kings County, Washington."); **Constance L. "Connie" Rice**, ("a prominent American civil rights activist and lawyer. She has received more than 50 major awards for her work in expanding opportunity and advancing multi-racial democracy."); **Bryan Stevenson**, (Founder and Executive Director, Equal Justice Initiative); **Roberto Villaseñor**, (former Tucson chief of police who once ordered his officers not to detain illegal aliens unless they had prior serious felony convictions, poses a threat to national security, or has gang affiliations). See a trend here? Where are the likes of former FBI Director Louis Freeh or any Republican representatives? And, if a fair and true commission should "look like America," how come there are so few Caucasians and no Conservatives on it?

Local police departments are being bullied into a "McDonaldsization" of policing as the result of onerous DOJ investigations and their resultant so-called "consent decrees." There is nothing consensual about a DOJ "consent decree." They come in and dictate to local departments every little detail of how they will do business. If the department or local government refuses to agree they are then hauled into federal court to the tune of hundreds of thousands if not millions of dollars of litigation costs. Local officials are left with the choice of standing up to and fighting the Federal leviathan (a fight they cannot possibly win even if they're in the right) or agreeing to the "consent decree." Such agreement brings federal meddling and involvement in every aspect of the operations and management of their local police department for years and years. Albuquerque Police Department recently had one of these 105-page abominations forced upon it by DOJ.

The other tactic employed by DOJ is to withhold precious grant monies to departments not willing to play ball by DOJ rules. This tactic works this way: the federal government collects local taxes from citizens and then doles it out back to local communities, with a cut taken off the top, to help fund the local police department's needs. If the locals don't cooperate, their "share" or "cut" goes elsewhere. How's that for a scam?

This one-sided shoving match must be stopped; else we end up with a national police force that tramples on the Constitution and ignores communities' and their citizens' individual viewpoints, pursuits, needs, and differences. Police tactics that are effective in New York City may not play out so well in parts of East Tennessee (or anywhere else citizens rightfully exercise their inherent God-given right to bear arms). This point alone is likely what was behind the aggressive approach and bullying undertaken by the Obama (in)Justice Department, as an unarmed populace is much more easily corralled into reeducation camps and gulags. Sounds paranoid? Consider that one US Attorney is seriously considering and has publicly discussed filing *criminal* charges against those that dare to question that penultimate Progressive shibboleth: climate change.[1]

Let us be perfectly clear, there are wonderful people working under the DOJ banner. The *specific* problem is a political one, often played out and enforced by DOJ's so-called Civil Rights Division, a purportedly apolitical organization. Woe to any department that comes under the scrutiny of that group of nincompoops. Look at the ridiculous, overbearing and ineffective pain that DOJ is inflicting upon departments from Washington State to Baltimore. DOJ's "consent decrees" have the unintended but logical and inevitable effect of causing violent crime rates to skyrocket, as they have in Baltimore. Criminals aren't stupid and they're well aware that when DOJ starts hassling their local police force the enforcement mechanisms become watered down. Like sunrise inevitably follows night, DOJ decrees inevitably lead to an increase in crime. DOJ should stop meddling in local affairs. Just as the Department of Education (another Federal power not enumerated in the Constitution) has FUBARed our Nation's school systems with their forced busing and politicized curriculum requirements, DOJ is now well on its way to destroying the concept of a local constabulary run and manned by Peace Officers.

Enough is enough. Under the Constitution and in accordance with American traditions of self-governance, policing is a matter best left to the states and municipalities. Unfortunately, it's obvious that few in the Obama administration are concerned about the Constitution, particularly many of those in his Justice Department. Interestingly, and with some degree of success, it is local sheriff's across America who see the danger; many of them having the moral courage to publicly stand up to the Feds when it comes to policing in their own backyards. Godspeed to them, as the true fight for America's soul may rest with them. Hopefully, Attorney General Sessions will put a stop to this out-of-control DOJ.

CHAPTER EIGHTEEN

OBAMA'S PUSILLANIMITY DEGRADED AMERICA'S VIRTUE

From Plato and Aristotle through the teachings of both the Old Testament and New Testament, right up to our Declaration of Independence, the classics teach us the importance of the moral virtues: courage, prudence, self-control and justice. This is what is known as character. Exhortation and growth of individual character, combined with humility, leads to magnanimity, a striving for greatness, in a society. Pusillanimity is the opposite of magnanimity. It is the depth of selfish character, which futility attempts to raise human choice above Divine direction. By his petulant acts and beliefs, Barack Obama consistently plumbed the depths of pusillanimity. A recent edict is a glaring example of his evil character.

In early 2016, Obama's Justice Department and Department of Education released a joint letter online to school systems around the nation, telling them they better open their restroom facilities to both genders, else face the wrath of the federal government. "There is no room in our schools for discrimination of any kind, including discrimination against transgender students on the basis of their sex," said Attorney General Loretta Lynch, in a written statement entitled " US

Departments of Justice and Education Release Joint Guidance to Help Schools Ensure the Civil Rights of Transgender Students."

The guidance makes clear that schools that receive federal funding cannot discriminate against transgender students based on Title IX of the Education Amendments of 1972. Lynch and Obama are lumping transgenders and other moral perverts in with that amendment's prohibition against discrimination based on sex. This argument is faulty on its face. God made men and women. Men have specific genetic coding and traits, as do women. Those, either due to mental illness or willful disobedience of God's choice, that attempt to call himself "she" (like Bruce Jenner) or herself "he" are no more entitled to protection under this law than would one who calls himself a beast be entitled to protection under SPCA laws!

But that logic aside, this governmental encroachment into what is inherently a parental and spiritual decision of each child and family is the truly dangerous act here. What Obama is saying is that parents can no longer teach their children that certain acts are inherently wrong. We have allowed our once-limited government to become arbiter of every nuance of daily life. And woes betide any individual who attempts to lead and teach a virtuous lifestyle. Now, not only will they face ridicule by fringe elements of society, like the radical lesbian, gay, queer, transgender, child molester groups, but now *punished* by their own federal government.

I will not sit idly by and watch America slouch toward Gomorrah, nor will many of my well-trained friends. But, taking our republic back by force would be a bloody business. Prayerfully, at some point before the republic reaches the tipping point we can partially right the ship so nearly foundered by the 44th occupant of the Oval Office. But, it will take courage and a degree of intestinal fortitude I fear the population lacks. Perhaps, Donald Trump's win in November 2016 signals otherwise.

Why do I say this? Typically, I do not watch television news programs. But, the deluge of 24/7 coverage after the Boston Marathon terror bombing forced me to observe a string of male and female news reporters saying how "scary" such events are, reinforcing the total lack of resiliency in our community. America has turned into a nation of wussies. Just a number of observations about the Marathon attack:

Two amateurish thugs set off improvised explosive devices at a large public gathering. Sadly, four people were killed and dozens injured. But, instead of rounding up a civilian posse, or at least telling folks to arm themselves and be on the lookout for the two thugs, the Boston Police Department told people to cower in their basements. And they did! This, from descendants of the likes of John Adams, Dr. Joseph Warren, Paul Revere, and Patrick Henry!

Massachusetts has already made it onerously difficult for law-abiding citizens to be armed, but the reaction of the majority of the populace was staggering in its implications. How long will it take before The West understands such panicking only reinforces our enemy (Islam)'s belief that we are a corpulent, wasted society?

Where were the men in Boston? Unfortunately, most of Obamanation is populated with males who would be scorned and laughed at by the men of the Greatest Generation of WWII. And I don't mean now as older men, but by their younger selves.

This is a pathetic state caused by the Left and mostly tolerated by the silent majority. Leftists love those that are helpless. If Americans weren't helpless enough to need Modernists, the Left would do everything and anything they could to undermine all that is good. Men, real men, are obstacles to their evil plan. There is now an entire generation of men in this country raised not to act in a crisis, but to call for help by dialing 911. I barely recognize my country.

CHAPTER NINETEEN

BLACK FEMALE WEST POINT CADETS: RAISED FISTS IN SALUTE TO WHAT?

WITH
JOHN TAYLOR

As reported on May 6, 2016 in a *The New York Times* article by Dave Philipps, "[A] group of young black women poised to graduate from the United States Military Academy gathered on the steps of that institution's oldest barracks last week in traditional gray dress uniforms, complete with sabers, for a group photograph. Known at West Point as an "Old Corps" photo because it mimics historical portraits, it was nearly identical to thousands that cadets have posed for over the decades, with one key difference: The 16 black women raised their clenched fists." As pointed out much later in the article, the clenched fist salute is the same on used by the radical Black Lives Matter crowd. Earlier in our republic's history, radicals like the Black Panthers and Malcolm X have used the clenched fist salute in furtherance of their violent, racist endeavors.

First, before exploring the underlying evils of such a gesture, one must ask, "Why were they gathering as "black females"? Any citizen might expect that these cadets had learned this important lesson in their four years of taxpayer-funded education: they are *not* black females, they are West Point cadets and future officers of the entire US Army, not *black* soldiers or *black* female soldiers.

The pose is unseemly at best. It is not a military unit or a platoon, company, or battalion of West Point cadets, and it is not a particular cadet group, like an athletic team or a club. It is a homogeneous group that obviously excludes people missing the same immutable genetic characteristics that they were born with by will of God.

People should not be excluded from such a photo because they are missing an immutable characteristic, rather because they don't belong to the group for failing to achieve or do what the group did, for example, achieve a varsity letter in lacrosse or other sport. Immutable characteristics are never a valid reason to exclude anyone in an Army whose only standard should be a measure of performance. For those reasons alone the photo is wrong. An exception to this, of course, is a photo taken of a group of friends. But, the raised fists belie friendship here. It is demonstrative of a gang or group dissatisfied with the larger, homogenous group of future military leaders.

Second, if these young ladies are not smart enough to realize and understand that this photo will engender discontent among many, to include members of the greater Army which they are about to join as leaders, then they shouldn't have been admitted to West Point in the first place. To state it more plainly, if they did not understand the problem here, then they were most likely too stupid to have been admitted to West

Point. It raises the specter of special treatment, a specter that unjustly taints other women and minorities that were admitted on true character and ability.

Lastly, such posturing based on race ignores the principles of virtuous leadership that strive for unit humility and magnanimity. The opposite of the selfish, pusillanimous actions displayed by those saying, "Look at me," solely because of the way God painted them. The sad racism displayed here would be obvious if it were a group of Caucasian cadets rendering a Nazi salute. There is no difference, except in the eyes of a subjective beholder or Progressive apologist for such small-minded and divisive behavior.

CHAPTER TWENTY

THE LGBT COWARDS
AT HARVARD UNIVERSITY

arvard University President Drew Gilpin Faust signed a letter endorsing a strategy proposed by another university official, Rakesh Khurana, which proposes that any student who belongs to an "unrecognized single-gender social organization" will "not be eligible to hold leadership positions in recognized student organizations or athletic teams." Khurana contends it's critical that Harvard students be in a community with multiple "genders, gender identity and sexual orientation."

Such is the state of postmodern Progressivism in the West. Not satisfied with the way and manner by which God has made man, these fools are displaying every manner of hubris by self-anointing themselves as anything but that sacred design. The absurdity of their acts would be pitiable if not for their demands that others not only affirm their profane acts but also associate with them by force.

So much for the constitutionally protected freedoms of association and free exercise of religion. These petulant monsters, in power because no workingman desires such position, need a good dose of violence leveled against them. Rakesh Khurana should be tarred and feathered, as the good people of Boston used to do in the Colonial days. Our children deserve no less a protective measure.

The days of peaceably resolving differences may be in the rearview mirror. In the span of two decades, except in a few rational states of the South and West, the cowards of the political class have caved in to the militant LGBT (Queer) demands. Rather than agree to live in and each to his own world, these evil creatures (Progressives, not the homosexuals) can't stand having any image around them that reflects or shows up their depravity. Just like gangsters get annoyed in the presence of goodness, these folks get angry when confronted with people who rationally point out the incongruity of such behavior. Sadly, they try to ally their cause with the immutable characteristics of race. But, homosexual behavior or a man dressing like a woman is behavior: a choice to offend the God who made them. They are free to disagree; but they are *not* free to force their viewpoints on the majority or our children.

CHAPTER TWENTY-ONE

WHEN MAN BEGINS TO CARE MORE ABOUT ANIMALS THAN HIS FELLOW MAN – ANOTHER EXAMPLE

Here is another example of the insanity in post-Modernity, where God and the creature He made in His image, man, are subjugated to the idols of the twenty-first century. In a story out of Liverpool, England, a lawsuit is in progress over whether a Staffordshire Terrier (read "Pit Bull") that ate part of its dead owner's body should be put down.

Despite the wishes of the dead man's family and the Merseyside Police, lawyers representing (you can't make this stuff up) "Freshfields Animal Rescue Centre and the Senior Staffy Club" appealed a court ruling that the animal, known as both Buster and Butch, should be destroyed following the grisly discovery last September, when the dog was found to have been feeding on the corpse of its dead owner.

"Dogs are scavengers by nature, but when they can't get food, they will get anything that is available to them," argued solicitor James Perry. No kidding, counselor. That is exactly why the animal needs to be destroyed. It has tasted and found liking human flesh.

Besides the overwhelming instances of this breed of dog killing or mauling humans, including infants and the elderly, dog apologists continue with their ridiculous claim that Pit Bulls are no more dangerous than other dogs. This, we suppose, is why one often finds poodles, collies and corgis in dog fighting pits around the world. But, as in every other issue where Liberal feelings are in play, facts take a second seat. "Poor, poor Butchy," they will caterwaul, "He was just being a dog." Exactly.

Why the West's courts entertain such junk lawsuits would be perplexing to my grandfather or any other rancher who had to put down a lame horse. Here, Butchy was more than lame. The police supported the owner's family's belief the dog posed a danger to the public. Merseyside police testified there was a "real risk that this dog, if rehoused, could harm a human being." Undoubtedly, the same Progressives who are fighting for this dangerous Pit Bull would cringe in terror at the thought of a firearms, "Guns (sibilant), Say what?"

This is what happens when what was once Christendom bans God from public debate (unless one is a Mohammedan, in which case English law now bows to Sharia). All of man's idols and fashions, animal rescues, abortion, sexual perversions, and addictions, become paramount to everything but the betterment and sanctity of human beings. If only unborn children had all the rights Butchy has had.

CHAPTER TWENTY-TWO

BALTIMORE'S "UPRISING" OF 2015

A George Soros-funded journalist, Evan Serpick, recently penned an opinion piece in *The Baltimore Sun* in which he called the 2015 Baltimore Riots an "Uprising." Here is a snippet of his analysis:

> *But just as often, young new leaders like Joseph Kent, Kwame Rose, Westley West and PFK Boom [sic] led the effort, and they brought other young people enjoying the new experience of speaking out about the deeply problematic conditions in their neighborhoods and their city.*

> *At the Western District headquarters, you could see young people challenging police officers they knew well from confrontations in the neighborhood. Others, there and elsewhere during these protests, spoke out about entrenched poverty, lack of economic opportunity, corrupt politicians, substandard housing, ineffective schools, white supremacy and racism. It was clear to anyone present that a social movement was emerging.*

One could write a book solely about all that is so evil and wrongheaded about Serpick's commentary, but my friend and first Patrol Sergeant, Jeff Rosen, the best law enforcement supervisor one could ask for, nailed it succinctly in his written response to this Fifth Columnist:

I read with bemused interest your Sun opinion piece about the Baltimore "uprising". Despite your prior employment as an editor at that storied edifice of journalism, The City Paper, I am not sure you have captured the meaning and connotation of the word. If I may, the following are uprisings in the true sense of the word, generally agreed upon by those with a grasp of history:

Warsaw, the 1943 ghetto uprising and the general uprising in 1945
Nat Turner slave revolt
Toussaint L'Overture and the slave revolt in Haiti
Storming the Bastille and the ensuing French Revolution

Hmmm, what do they have in common? All were violent responses to overwhelmingly oppressive situations. These involved horrific physical and institutional acts that were beyond conscience, demanding an overwhelming and violent response. If you truly believe that the plight of black folks in Baltimore falls within the same parameters, you need a checkup from the neck up. Are SRB and the City leadership playing by the same rules as Hitler or Louis XVI? Are Baltimore residents of Sandtown-Winchester channeling slaves in Virginia or Haiti? I think not. Get a grip on your common sense and rhetoric. Surely widespread problems exist in Baltimore. Rioting, arson and felony theft are not political acts or necessary violence fueled by inhuman treatment. I see that your new employer is funded by George Soros, a convicted felon. That pretty much explains it all. There is none so blind as he who will not see.

Jeff last hit on a particularly sore point concerning the entire Black LIES Matter crowd that many cowardly politicians and police leaders have ignored. The entire movement is based on a lie. Black hoodlums, not police, are responsible for the overwhelming number of shooting deaths in the community. Courage may require one to speak out against voguish but evil spirits of the times; impure conduct or trends; and, the common tendency to seek the path of least resistance. It also requires one to speak the truth even if doing so may be personally painful:

"For if we sin willfully after that we have received the knowledge of the truth, there remaineth no more sacrifice for sins"

—Hebrews 10:26.

Scripture also speaks to those who "are willingly ignorant" (2 Peter 3:5). The meaning is the same. It is one thing to be unaware of the truth; it is altogether different when people know what is true, yet ignore it out of cowardice or political expediency. No doubt, many of the poor people in Baltimore are woefully ignorant. Evan Serpick, like his puppet master Soros, is willfully so: so shame on him.

The truth of the entire Black Lives Matter is brilliantly exposed by Urey Patrick and John C. Hall in the 3rd edition of their classic *In Defense of Self and Others . . . Issues, Facts*

& Fallacies—The Realities of Law Enforcement's Use of Deadly Force. Relying solely on law enforcement reports and grand jury testimony from African-American citizens of Ferguson and the Department of Justice's investigation, these two retired Supervisory Special Agents of the FBI nail it. Their book ought to be required reading for every prosecutor, criminal defense counsel, police supervisor and trainer, and judge who dares to second guess officers' decisions made under situations that are "tense, uncertain and rapidly evolving."[1]

In spite of these truths about Black Lives Matter, many major city police departments continue to cater to these domestic terrorists. In Baltimore, my hometown and where I started my law enforcement career, the cowards in its police department recently suspended a former shift mate and colleague of mine for simply calling Black Lives Matter "thugs," which by any reasonable measure they are!

CHAPTER TWENTY-THREE

THE LOST ART OF VIRTUE: LYING AS AN ART FORM IN THE MILITARY

I n 2015, the *Strategic Studies Institute and US Army War College Press* published an article, "Lying to Ourselves: Dishonesty in the Army Profession" by Dr. Leonard Wong, PhD and Dr. Stephen J. Gerras, PhD, both respected professors at the Army War College and retired military officers. Having worked with them on the faculty at Carlisle Barracks, home of the Army War College, their contributions to the profession of arms are monumentally good and true. Their article should be mandatory reading for officers at the tactical, operational and strategic levels of command.

Sadly, however, the US Army War College would do well to begin looking within its own halls for officially sanctioned lying. In November 2013, during Thanksgiving holiday, one of the college's lesser deans took it upon himself, like a thief in the night, to remove all of the paintings depicting any Confederate general or hero from the walls of Root Hall. When immediately called on it by *The Washington Times* that Sunday, the Army War College leadership went into dishonest overdrive. They called a retired colonel, who was acting as the head of building services, to perform an "inventory" of the art objects. When the retired colonel told the leadership, "I just did one last month," they said, "Do another one. NOW!" Later that afternoon, the Public Affairs Office told *The Washington Times*, "No, this rearrangement of artwork was done as the result of an inventory we are currently performing, there's nothing else to it." And the 2-star General who was then the commandant, who must or should have known this to be a complete falsehood, held to that lie.

The colonel who removed the artwork depicting such famous military tacticians as Robert E. Lee, J. E. B. Stuart and Thomas J. "Stonewall" Jackson, is apparently intellectually incapable of thinking out of time. He wrongfully and hatefully imposed his own modern notions of right and wrong on Civil War participants, calling Lee and others "traitors." In the summer of 2009, prior to assuming duties as a member of the faculty in the Department of National Security & Strategy, I personally attended a three-week instructor prep course with this offending individual. I found his lack of mental agility and prejudice against historical figures from the South disconcerting then; and, even more so now. He fails to acknowledge what President Dwight D. Eisenhower did in 1960, when responding to the concerns of a citizen criticizing the former five-star Commander of Supreme Headquarters Allied Forces Europe (SHAFE) in WWII for his oft-spoken praise of Robert E. Lee:

August 9, 1960

Dear Dr. Scott:

Respecting your August 1 inquiry calling attention to my often expressed admiration for General Robert E. Lee, I would say, first, that we need to understand that at the time of the War between the States the issue of secession had remained unresolved for more than 70 years. Men of probity, character, public standing and unquestioned loyalty, both North and South, had disagreed over this issue as a matter of principle from the day our Constitution was adopted.

General Robert E. Lee was, in my estimation, one of the supremely gifted men produced by our Nation. He believed unswervingly in the Constitutional validity of his cause which until 1865 was still an arguable question in America; he was a poised and inspiring leader, true to the high trust reposed in him by millions of his fellow citizens; he was thoughtful yet demanding of his officers and men, forbearing with captured enemies but ingenious, unrelenting and personally courageous in battle, and never disheartened by a reverse or obstacle. Through all his many trials, he remained selfless almost to a fault and unfailing in his faith in God. Taken altogether, he was noble as a leader and as a man, and unsullied as I read the pages of our history.

From deep conviction, I simply say this: a nation of men of Lee's calibre would be unconquerable in spirit and soul. Indeed, to the degree that present-day American youth will strive to emulate his rare qualities, including his devotion to this land as revealed in his painstaking efforts to help heal the Nation's wounds once the bitter struggle was over, we, in our own time of danger in a divided world, will be strengthened and our love of freedom sustained.

Such are the reasons that I proudly display the picture of this great American on my office wall.

Sincerely,
Dwight D. Eisenhower

The Army War College would serve itself well by removing faculty incapable of separating their personal prejudices of the Civil War from the realities of history and the perspective of the time. Taking the perspective of those living through an historic event and ignoring the benefit of 20-20 hindsight demands the kind of flexible, elastic and deep thinking intellect we want educating our military officers.

Officers who only view history through the skewed lens of 20/20 hindsight are frankly not smart enough to be teaching military personnel who are expected to think and act at the strategic level. This particular officer ought to remember that it was Abraham Lincoln who suspended the right of habeas corpus and unlawfully imprisoned thousands of US citizens in violation of the very Constitution he swore to uphold and defend and in defiance of rulings from the Supreme Court of the United States. The states that seceded did so from a voluntary compact amongst several states. In fact, our nation was once known as "These United States of America" instead of "The Unites States." In light of history, it was Lincoln, not Robert E. Lee and his generals, who was a traitor to the rule of law and our republic's founding documents.

But, that argument is best left to the dustbins of history where we can *learn* from it in an effort to improve our diverse lots in life. Instead, unable to think out of time, this officer took it upon himself to impose his queer notions of history upon others. Strikingly, when his sins were brought to light, instead of correcting him, the Army War College's leadership chose the path of lies to cover up his treachery. Fixing integrity problems starts locally. It is deeply saddening that the alma mater to many of us has, to date, not righted this egregious wrong.

As a seeming endless stream of investigations have uncovered of late, Carlisle is hardly alone in this respect. Accordingly, every command would be better off by instilling the cardinal virtues of moral courage, competency, self-control and justice at the local level. If this balance is demanded and sustained by leadership at the tactical, operational and strategic levels, our military will retain that sacred honor our citizenry deserves and expects. And, we might produce general and flag officers with enough stomach to tell their political masters "No" when those masters try and impose policy that is morally abhorrent and damaging to our war fighting capabilities.

CHAPTER TWENTY-FOUR

OVER, BUT,
"WHAT DIFFERENCE WILL IT MAKE?"

Barack Hussein Obama's administration was the most damaging in our republic's relatively brief history. Earlier in 2016, when talking with a young member of the Republican establishment, he asked, "Why do you think Trump is resonating with voters?" In reply, I pointed out, "Well, I can't speak for everyone, but many of us are personally really pissed that after fiscally supporting Republican candidates in 2014, the House and Senate with Republican majorities have done nothing to defund Obama's unconstitutional agenda." This young man's reply is what is most distressing. He said that the Republican Congress do not want to limit the president's powers for when it is "their turn!"

So, instead of having the moral courage to abide by their oath to uphold and defend the Constitution of the United States, the Republican Party may be more interested in crass political power, unleashing an even more powerful presidency that will further unbalance our once treasured Executive-Legislative-Judicial balance of powers. Instead of asserting their Constitutional power and responsibility over the purse, they have set up a future whereby alternating presidents will whipsaw our populace with evermore encroaching Executive Orders. Such is the way of a dictatorship, not the sacred method of government so brilliantly envisioned by Jefferson, Madison, and Adams and valiantly fought for by Washington and his troops.

As a lifelong Republican now living in the Peoples Republic of Delaware, I am used to not having my voice heard by my senators and congressmen. But, at a national level, I rejoiced in 2014 when we leveraged control of the House and Senate. Sadly, the likes of crying John Boehner, who did nothing to derail Obamacare and other overreaching and intrusive Federal programs, quickly extinguished all my joy. At times, Paul Ryan proved no better.

So, yes, I am really pissed at the Republican establishment. They have proven themselves to be nothing more than just a different flavor of excessive Federal governance. So pissed that I voted for and fiscally supported Donald Trump, especially when the Party leadership attempted to play games with the electoral process.

Americans are getting fed up with a federal government that hamstrings our corporations and small businesses with obscenely complicated and onerous tax, EPA and OSHA rules. There is a brewing and strong undercurrent of discontent over the breadth and depth of government. When law enforcement non-judicial asset forfeiture schemes (where police seize cash from citizens absent any nexus to a crime and then say 'prove it is yours') takes in more money than all of the burglaries nationwide every year, something is rotten. Some states now have a device in their state patrol cars that can steal money from people's credit and debit cards absent any probable cause!

If we do not fix this peaceably, things may get a bit nastier than Baltimore or Ferguson. Again every citizen and certainly every politician ought to read John Ross's *Unintended Consequences* to get a clue of what I am talking about. For, if it comes time to "feed the hogs" the nabobs in DC might become the first on the feed list.

CHAPTER TWENTY-FIVE

NO EXPERIENCE OR JUSTICE IN THE MILITARY -A LONG TIME IN THE MAKING

WITH
JOHN TAYLOR

Early in 2015, at Minot Air Force Base, in exchange for TSgt Michael T. Maher's plea of guilty to three counts and multiple specifications of sexual abuse of a child in violation of Article 120b of the Uniform Code of Military Justice, prosecutors and the command accepted a pre-trial agreement limiting Maher's term of confinement to 10 years' imprisonment. The details of the case are too disgusting to print in detail, but suffice to say 35-year-old Mayer specifically instructed a child to expose her genitals and rear end and he then penetrated them in extraordinarily vulgar ways. As fathers, police officers and former prosecutors, there are insufficient words to express our rage at such conduct. Twenty years would have been a light sentence if either of us was on the bench and we suspect a panel (military jury) would have given him more.

Why are we focusing on this gruesome although, sadly, not particularly rare offense? Because, at the same base, the Air Force was seeking over 130 years of charges against another noncommissioned officer, TSgt Aaron D. Allmon, for trying to pick up women while working in the public affairs office! It has been reported that the prosecutorial zeal in this case was so great that an Air Force officer appointed to investigate the case said the piled-up charges were combined to "artificially exaggerate the criminality of the accused," who often was simply "socially maladroit and crass."

Where, we ask, is such prosecutorial zeal for animals such as Maher or, in the Army's case, a traitor like Sergeant Bergdahl who walked away from his combat station in Afghanistan, directly causing the loss of life of fellow Soldiers? The Investigating Officer in the latter case recommended a Special Court-Martial for Bergdahl, de jure limiting his exposure to a possible maximum of six months incarceration.

While every generation may remember the good old days with nostalgia and sneer at the seeming ineptitude of the current generation, the fact remains that the collective Judge Advocate General's (JAG) Corps of each service has strayed from its primary mission: enforcing discipline through a swift and effective criminal justice system. Since the drawdown of the Nineties, which left each service's The Judge Advocate General (JAG ... the then two-star senior attorney of each service) scrambling to protect their own personnel end strength, JAGs began branching out into myriad arcane specialties. We now have environmental, contract, personnel, and administrative and operational law specialties. In the interim, the position of trial counsel (prosecutor) and defense counsel got kicked to the curb.

When the authors were senior captains in Germany in the mid-90s, it was not uncommon for one defense counsel to have at least two or three general courts-martial a month on their dockets. This, in addition to the dozens of non-judicial punishment (Article 15s) and lesser levels of courts-martial in a fast-paced world of keeping young, often drunken off-duty Soldiers in line. It was not uncommon for one trial counsel to try a dozen contested (non-plea) cases a year and literally ten times that many plea agreements. Additionally, being a trial counsel was the sine qua non of being a successful captain of judge advocates. There was a constant pressure to succeed and plenty of experience at the end of the pipeline. The military judges trying our cases had an exponentially larger caseload when they were young captains in the early 80s. Not anymore, and we are witnessing, these two cases are perfect exemplars, the decline and fall of effective performance of the main statutory mission of the services' JAG Corps: the commander's tool to enforce discipline in our Army, Navy, Marine Corps, and Air Force.

The last important issue to consider is the politicization of criminal justice. For instance, Major Jamie Humphries, a Minot public affairs officer, said the Air Force does not tolerate any form of sexual harassment. "Sexual harassment or assault of any kind in our service is unacceptable and simply not tolerated," he said. So, we are now disproportionately focusing and overcharging simple harassment cases (mala prohibita crimes) to the exclusion of true mala in se crimes (crimes that are considered wrong in and of themselves).

Judge advocates tout themselves as the conscience of the command, supposedly acting as a buffer between political outrage and the administration of justice. Now, they have become incendiary material to the flames of political correctness and the victims of true crimes like sexual child abuse, forcible rape and aggravated assault are left in the embers. The various deleterious effects of the liberal progressive agenda on our military are plain for all to see. This is one.

CHAPTER TWENTY-SIX

USE OF FORCE – LAW & SCRIPTURE ON THE INHERENT, GOD-GIVEN RIGHT OF SELF-DEFENSE

A solid theory of war or force is rooted in two principles: (1) the United States' national interest must retain its primacy over the collective goals of the international community; and, (2) self-defense, individual, collective, or anticipatory, must be the cause of *any* use of force. From these principles, America should gauge the scope, amount and duration of its application of military force necessary to reach its enduring goals of security, prosperity and preservation of American values rooted in our Constitution. At a personal level as virtuous men and women, we must understand our responsibilities and duties to protect the innocent and ourselves. Once clearly stated, both our adversaries and our allies will know our intent and resolve. The desired result is a not so fragile peace and a more secure world marketplace for commerce, ideas, and spiritual freedoms.

NATIONAL INTEREST

It is her national interest that gives America the will to fight. Sun Tzu observed that national unity was an essential requirement of victorious war.[1] Many in the European Union (EU) and the United Nations (UN) derisively refer to America as a nation of "cowboys."[2] America's economic and social strengths derive from precisely the fact that it is not a parliamentary European Union-like entity, but rather a free market society unafraid of being a cowboy.

If America cedes its core values and security to a conglomerate of diverse, international interests, it risks diminishing its power and sovereignty to the point of becoming a second-tier voice in a parliamentary aggregate slouching toward socialistic mediocrity. Sir Winston Churchill once stated, "The greatest vice of capitalism is the unequal sharing of blessings, while the greatest virtue of socialism is the equal sharing of miseries."[3] As such, America spiritual and economic engine must run on the fuel of free market economics, respect and integrity of private property rights, and security from external threats. As so brilliantly explained by author Tom Bethell in *The Noblest Triumph: Property and Prosperity Through the Ages*, "When property is privatized, and the rule of law is established, in such a way that *all* including the rulers themselves are subject to the same law, economies will prosper and civilization will blossom. Of the different possible configurations of property, only *private* property can have this desirable effect." (Emphasis added)

Threats to the United States today and into the foreseeable future recognize that America's center of gravity is the strength of our free market economy and our constitutional republican form of limited government: we are not a democracy, where the tyranny of the mobs rules. The primacy of these national interests as the foundation of our societal will to fight must be protected.

As exemplified by many modern theorists and legal scholars,[4] many are stridently pushing America to the brink of subservience to the United Nations or some similar "supernumerary" power. While such international organizations have utility in reaching accords concerning aviation, laws of the sea, and similar treaties and agreement relating to free trade and commerce, they should *never* reach a level of primacy over America's core Constitutional principles. "Do not let spacious plans for a new world divert your energies from saving what is left of the old."[5]

Moreover, when one recognizes that many of the decision-makers and precedent-setters on the International criminal court[6] are from countries and cultures that may not routinely respect the rule of law, more less American Constitutional principles; it would be sheer folly for the United States to cede its National Interest to such a tribal tribunal. On the individual, will to fight level, our Soldiers should never be subjected to such a spectacle without full Constitutional protections.

The importance and primacy of national interest cannot be overemphasized. People fight for what is close and dear to them. As a corollary to this, Sir Winston noted that when one attempts to decipher the intent of another country – adversary or ally – one should look to that country's national interest. "I cannot forecast to you the action of Russia. It is a riddle wrapped in a mystery inside an enigma: but perhaps there is a key. That key is Russian national interest."[7]

SELF-DEFENSE

As Winston Churchill put it, "One ought never to turn one's back on a threatened danger and try to run away from it.

If you do that, you will double the danger. But if you meet it promptly and without flinching, you will reduce the danger by half. Never run away from anything. Never!"[8]

The lawful authority, both domestic and international, for the United States to use force is most emphatically rooted in the right of self-defense. By keeping all uses of military power – specifically war and war-like actions – founded in self-defense, America will retain the moral high ground, clearly signal its strategic intentions to potential adversaries, and avoid straying into the morass of commitments not rooted in self-defense.[9] This extends to one's personal right of self-defense.

In order to appreciate to depth and breadth of the right of self-defense, it is worth examining its historical roots. Consistently, since at least 60 BC, laws and customs have recognized individuals' inherent right to reasonably defend their selves from an attacker threatening to inflict death or serious bodily injury. Historically, the right of self-defense has been viewed not as a statutory or legal right, but as a divine natural right permanently bestowed upon all persons by virtue of existence. Over 2,000 years ago Markus Tullius Cicero wrote:

> [T]here does exist therefore, gentlemen, a law which is a law not of the statute-book, but of nature; a law which we possess not by instruction, tradition, or reading, but which we have caught, imbibed, and sucked in at Nature's own breast; a law which comes to us not by education but by constitution, not by training but by intuition—the law, I mean, that should our life have fallen into any snare, into the violence and the weapons of robbers or foes, every method of winning a way to safety would be morally justifiable.[10]

In AD 529, the Roman scholar Justinian observed, "that which someone does for the safety of his body, let it be regarded as having been done legally."[11] The Old Testament provides, "If a thief be found breaking up, and be smitten that he die, there shall be no bloodshed for him. If the sun be risen upon him, there shall be bloodshed for him."[12]

William Blackstone, the father of English common law, wrote, "[s]elf defense is justly called the primary law of nature, so it is not, neither can it be in fact, taken away by the laws of society."[13] "The right of having and using arms for self-preservation and defense" is one of the five auxiliary rights people possess to "protect and maintain 'the three great and primary rights' personal security, personal liberty, and private property."[14]

Sir Michael Foster went further, observing in the *Crown Cases*,

[t]he right of self-defence [sic] in these cases is founded in the law of nature, and is not, nor can be, superseded by any law of society. For before societies were formed for mutual defence and preservation, the right of self-defence resided in individuals; it could not reside elsewhere, and since in cases of necessity, individuals incorporated into society cannot resort for protection to the law of society, that law with great propriety and strict justice considereth them, as still, in that instance, under the protection of the law of nature.[15]

English philosopher John Locke observed, "self defense is a part of the law or nature, nor can it be denied the community, even against the king himself."[16] In his treatise on civil government, self-defense is fundamental to the very existence of mankind. Much like one is justified in killing a wild animal if it displayed intent to attack; one is justified in taking the life of another person if that person displayed intent to do harm to you. Locke reasoned:

> *[i]t being reasonable and just, I should have a right to destroy that which threatens me with destruction: for, by the fundamental law of nature, man being to be preserved as much as possible, when all cannot be preserved, the safety of the innocent is to be preferred: and one may destroy a man who makes war upon him, or has discovered an enmity to his being, for the same reason that he may kill a wolf or a lion; because such men are not under the ties of the common law of reason, have no other rule, but that of force and violence, and so may be treated as beasts of prey, those dangerous and noxious creatures, that will be sure to destroy him whenever he falls into their power.*

Like Locke, St. Thomas Aquinas believed self-defense derived from natural law, but defined self-defense not based on the assailant's act, but the defender's intent. He reasoned that one acts in self-defense where his intent is not to cause harm, but to preserve his own life. The other person may be harmed, but that is a product of the innocent defender's intent, which was to prevent the attacker from causing him harm.

> *[K]illing one's assailant is justified provided one does not intend to kill him. Nothing hinders one act from having two effects, only one of which is intended, while the other is beside the intention. Accordingly, the act of self-defense may have two effects; one, the saving of one's life; the other, the slaying of the aggressor. Therefore, this act, since one's intention is to save one's own life, is not unlawful, seeing*

that is natural to everything to keep itself in being as far as possible. [17]

Our American system of government is based upon enumerated rights and responsibilities set forth in the US Constitution. To the founding fathers, the right to self-defense was not only constitutional, but pre-existed the Constitution. They believed it was an inherent, natural God-given right that no man could take away. Self-defense sits at the heart of the rights protected by the Constitution: the right to life.

To understand the Constitution, and what its authors intended, Thomas Jefferson said "[o]n every question of construction [of the Constitution] let us carry ourselves back to the time when the Constitution was adopted, recollect the spirit manifested in the debates, and instead of trying what meaning may be squeezed out of the text, or invent against it, conform to the probable one in which it was passed." [18]

It is for this reason, too, that America must not succumb to the temptation of moral or legal relativism or equivalency with other nations' laws. On such fundamental concerns as self-defense, America may enter into short or long-term alliances, but must not submit to the will of the collective international masses when discerning what constitutes a justifiable act of self-defense.

The founding fathers used English common law as a platform to build the US Constitution. English common law long recognized individual right to self-defense as a natural and divine right. [19] The drafters were heavily influenced by the works of William Blackstone, and drafted the core of the Constitution to protect life, liberty and property. In Blackstone's *Commentaries on the Laws of England*, Blackstone held that the three primary rights protected by English law were the rights of personal security, personal liberty, and private property. Self-defense was a part of the right to personal security, as one could not be secure in their safety without the right to defend against those wishing to deprive him of it.[20]

Mirroring Blackstone's statements, Samuel Adams wrote, "[A]mong the natural rights of the Colonists are these: First, a right to life; Secondly, to liberty; Thirdly, to property; together with the right to support and defend them in the best manner they can."[21] The Constitution reflects Blackstone's influence in the Bill of Rights, which explicitly protects our rights to life, liberty, and property, and freedom from governmental intrusion.

Even under international constructs, it should be noted that customary and statutory international law recognizes the inherent right of self-defense. The application of anticipatory or pre-emptive self-defense and the maxim of a person's inherent right to self-defense were firmly established in the *Caroline* incident. In 1837, the British were fighting a counter-insurgency war along the Niagara River in Canada. Insurgents on both the American and British sides of the river were using the steamer *Caroline*. On the evening of December 29, 1837, British combatants crossed onto the American side of the river and destroyed the *Caroline* while it was docked in Schlosser, New York. The Americans protested, but the British responded that they were merely exercising their inherent right of self-defense. American Secretary of State Daniel Webster disagreed. In response to Lord Ashburton's claim that the British acted in self-defense, Webster declared that for an act to be self-defense, it "must be a necessity of self-defense, instant, overwhelming, leaving no choice of means and no moment for deliberation."[22]

Secondly, to be appropriate, self-defense must be proportional, not "unreasonable or excessive." While never admitting culpability for the *Caroline* incident, the British apologized to the United States for the incident.

In 1928, Secretary of State Frank Kellogg, author of the Kellogg-Brian Pact (also known as the Pact of Paris), said, "The right of self defense is inherent in every sovereign state and is implicit in every treaty. Every nation is free at all times and regardless of treaty provisions to defend its territory from attack or invasion and it alone is competent to decide whether circumstances require recourse to war in self defense."[23] The Pact of Paris renounced war as a mechanism to resolve international disputes, and later served as the basis for the charge of crimes against peace prosecuted against the Nazi war criminals at the Nuremberg International Military Tribunal following World War II. Kellogg recognized that a sovereign nation, by means of its individuals, has an inherent right to defend itself from outside aggressions, and that right was neither created by, nor can be abrogated by, written international law or treaty.

The International Military Tribunal reaffirmed Daniel Webster's definition of self-defense when ruling that the German invasion of Norway in 1940 was not defensive because it was unnecessary to prevent an "imminent" Allied invasion. The Tribunal echoed Webster's criteria for self-defense, stating, "preventative action in foreign territory is justified only in case of an instant and overwhelming necessity for self-defense, leaving no choice of means, and no moment of deliberation."

It is this last limitation in international law, however, that mandates that America must be unfettered in developing its own policy dealing with pre-emptive self-defense. As discussed below, a fair reading of the UN Charter also limits America's ability to conduct pre-emptive, unilateral acts of self-defense. Hence, America's right to self-defense should not always be fettered by these constraints: her National Interest may supersede the International consensus, yet her right to respond remains consistent with a self-defense theory or justification. This is especially true when preemptive actions or predicated on open and fair warning to potential adversaries (such as the Taliban's failure to relinquish al Qaeda).

The United Nations was founded to provide a forum in which international disputes could be resolved without resorting to armed force.[24] The United Nation's goal was to substitute a community response for unilateral action in deterring aggression. At the core of the Charter of the United Nations is a prohibition of use of force absent authorization from the Security Council, a body created by the United Nations to oversee international peace.[25] Article 2(4) of the UN Charter provides: "[a]ll Members shall refrain in their international relations from the threat or use of force against the territorial integrity or political independence of any state, or in any other manner inconsistent with the purposes of the United Nations."[26] The Charter provided two express exceptions to the prohibition on use of force. Article 42 provides that that the Security Council may vote to authorize military force to restore peace.

And most importantly, Article 51 recognizes:

Nothing in the present Charter shall impair the inherent right of individual or collective self defense if an armed attack occurs against a Member of the United Nations until the Security Council has taken the measures necessary to maintain international peace and security. Measures taken by Members in the exercise of the right of self defense shall be immediately reported to the Security Council and shall not in any way affect the authority and responsibility of the Security Council under the present Charter to take at any time such action as it deems necessary in order to maintain or restore international peace and security.

Just as the United States Constitution did not create or confer any rights, but merely recognized God-given, inherent right under Natural Law, UN Charter Article 51 did not *create* a new right, it merely codified the pre-existing right all individuals have to self-defense.[27] Article 51 also codified the customary international law that existed at time the charter was adopted. At the time, self-defense was defined in terms of the standard set forth in *Caroline* and the application of that standard during the 1946 International Military Tribunal at Nuremberg; necessity and proportionality.

Across the mission spectrum, from humanitarian relief operations to force-on-force conflict, America can justly and lawfully support uses of force in self-defense. But, as an extension of the international law set forth in Article 51, America should retain the ability to unilaterally conduct more robust preemptive, anticipatory acts.

This especially true when countering rogue or stateless terrorists in possession of Weapons of Mass Destruction (WMD). This last point is clearly enunciated in The 2006 National Security Strategy of the United States (NSS):

The greater the threat, the greater is the risk of inaction, and the more compelling the case for taking anticipatory action to defend ourselves, even if uncertainty remains as to the time and place of the enemy's attack. There are few greater threats than a terrorist attack with WMD. To forestall or prevent such hostile acts by our adversaries, the United States will, if necessary, act preemptively in exercising our inherent right of self-defense.[28]

Lastly, a just theory of war will help ensure that the will of the American people will remain steadfast behind any war effort undertaken. War itself is too full of chance and uncertainty to embark upon without such strong support. Again, Winston Churchill understood this when in *My Early Life: A Roving Commission*, he said,

Never, never, never believe any war will be smooth and easy, or that anyone who embarks on the strange voyage can measure the tides and hurricanes he will encounter. The statesman who yields to war fever must realise that once the signal is given, he is no longer the master of policy but the slave of unforeseeable and uncontrollable events. Antiquated War Offices, weak, incompetent, or arrogant Commanders, untrustworthy allies, hostile neutrals, malignant Fortune, ugly surprises, awful miscalculations — all take their seats at the Council Board on the morrow of a declaration of war. Always remember, however sure you are that you could easily win, that there would not be a war if the other man did not think he also had a chance.

Lastly, as far as civil law is concerned, law enforcement rarely prevents crimes from happening. Mostly, they are report writers and criminal investigators who seek justice after the fact. The law repeatedly recognizes this fact: "[t]here is no constitutional right to be protected by the state against being murdered."[29]

SELF-DEFENSE IN SCRIPTURE
Old Testament

Exodus 22:2–3 tells us, "If the thief is found breaking in, and he is struck so that he dies, there shall be no guilt for his bloodshed. If the sun has risen on him, there shall be guilt for his bloodshed. He should make full restitution; if he has nothing, then he shall be sold for his theft."

Threats at night are especially onerous; hence, burglary is a specially defined felony as breaking into the dwelling house of another with the intent to commit a felony. Under such circumstances and great potential for threat to life, lethal force is excusable. During the daytime, when threats are more easily distinguished, folks can recognize and later apprehend a thief if he escapes. No *personal* property is worth killing someone over.

In the Sixth Commandment told Moses, "Thou shalt not murder," rather than "Thou shalt not kill." This is an important distinction that has been lost in translation. Proverbs 25:26 reads, "A righteous man who falters before the wicked is like a murky spring and a polluted well." Personally, there would be no greater act of cowardice and shame if I failed to stop wicked simply because I chose to be unarmed and unable to stop a deranged killer at Mass.

Psalm 144:1 states, "Who trains my hand for war and my fingers for battle."

NEW TESTAMENT

First Timothy 5:8 tells us, "But if anyone does not provide for his own, and especially for those of his household, he has denied the faith and is worse that an unbeliever." This defines personal responsibility to me. There is a distinction between the woefully ignorant and the willfully ignorant, Second Peter 3:5, which speaks of those who "willingly forget." Some prefer the King James translation, which says, "they are willingly ignorant." The meaning is the same. It is one thing to be unaware of the truth; it is altogether different when people are "willingly ignorant."

See also, Hebrews 10:26,
"For if we sin willfully after that we have received the knowledge of the truth, there remaineth no more sacrifice for sins"
Matthew 4:7,
"It is written again, 'You shall not tempt the Lord your God.'"

As a member of Opus Dei (God's Work), I believe that our Creator expects to work and be as self-sufficient as possible in order to care for our families and others less fortunate.

This faulty notion of "Let Go, Let God" is careless and irresponsible. When Satan was tempting Jesus in the wilderness, he challenged the Lord to throw himself off the top of the temple. Satan reasoned that God's angels would protect him. Jesus responded: "It is written again, 'You shall not tempt the Lord your God.'"

Use of force in self-defense during an actual attack or imminent attack is far different from taking vengeance upon another *after* the fact. Scripture clearly places that in the exclusive domain of God (Romans 12:19), who delegates such authority to the state, which, as we find in Romans 13:4, "is God's minister to you for good. But if you do evil, be afraid; for he does not bear the sword in vain; for he is God's minister, an avenger to execute wrath on him who practices evil."

Christ's rebuke of St. Peter, who used a sword to cut off the ear of Malchus (a servant of the high priest in the company of a detachment of troops sent to arrest the Lord), is often used by pacifists to deny the individual right of self-defense. However, a full reading of what Christ said to Peter puts this phrase in proper perspective: "Put your sword in its place, for all who take the sword will perish by the sword. Or do you think that I cannot now pray to My Father, and He will provide Me with more than twelve legions of angels? How then could the Scriptures be fulfilled, that it must happen thus?" (Matthew 26:52-54).

Jesus told Peter to "put your sword in its place" rather than "get rid of it." Peter's–and our–sword (or weapon) was to protect his own mortal life from danger. The Lord God and Creator did not need Peter's sword for protection!

Many pacifists believe that Christ was somehow the world's first hippie, a nice, longhaired peacenik that would roll over at the first hint of danger. How arrogant and presumptuous is that view! It is using the power and strength of our Creator to excuse cowardice and inaction. led, that it must happen thus?

Lastly, in the parable of the Good Samaritan, Jesus referred to the Old Testament summary of all the laws of the Bible into two great commandments: "'You shall love the Lord your God with all your heart, with all your soul, with all your strength, and with all your mind, and your neighbor as yourself" (Luke 10:25–37).

It was the Good Samaritan who took care of the mugging victim who was a neighbor to the victim. The others who walked by and ignored the victim's plight were not acting as neighbors to him. Similarly, we ought not leave our neighbors, colleagues, and fellow parishioners in the lurch. Just as we fight to protect the Right to Life of the unborn, we must fight to protect the lives of the innocent already born.

So, what does all of the foregoing have to do with the dangers of Modernity? Well, its dangers are two-fold: subsuming America's national interests to supernumerary authority like the United Nations (the penultimate Progressive wet dream); and, trying to eliminate or severely limit our inherent God-given right of individual self-defense (specifically the right to bear arms). The latter is a right hanging in a 5–4 balance of the *Heller* decision.[30] Prayerfully, Donald Trump's inauguration will shore up *Heller* for the few decades.

CHAPTER TWENTY-SEVEN

THE PHARAOH STRIKES AGAIN - RENAMING MOUNT MCKINLEY

As schoolchildren, we memorized many points of geography, one of them the highest mountain in the United States: Mount McKinley in Alaska. Towards the end of his second term, Barack Hussein Obama (aka The Pharaoh) changed the name of that famous mountain to "Denali." Now, I had always thought a Denali was a high-end GMC SUV named after the Alaskan region in which Mount McKinley is located. But, since the Pharaoh has refused to acknowledge that the cowboys (and that the US Cavalry) beat the Indians, this is just one of his many attempts to scour America's historical walls of anything that does not fit his Socialist and anti-Colonial worldview.

Just as Stalin did in the USSR, Obama has done everything within his power (and outside his enumerated powers) to change our historical narrative. He returned a bust of Winston Churchill to the British Embassy; he has flown the national colors at half-mast for homosexuals and pop singers (but not heroes like SEAL Chris Kyle); and, called to congratulate gay NBA players, while ignoring the death of countless warriors.

The Pharaoh is nothing short of a tyrant that needed to be toppled by any means. The notion that "he only has X number of months left in office" should not have been reason to celebrate. As his political days drew to a close, his dangerousness increased. He was looking to create a meaningful legacy. Unfortunately for the republic, it is not a legacy steeped in the Constitution or the American way.

Urge all patriots to continue to call Mount McKinley by that proper and fitting name. Refuse to bend to his evil will and leave him with the legacy he deserves: the worst president in our nation's history, bar none. He makes Abraham Lincoln look like a Constitutionalist and Jimmy Carter a genius.

The days of this Pharaoh were limited, thank God, by the terms of our Constitution. We all might have prayed harder, though, that he succumbed to the bite of an asp before his time in office expired. It would have been nothing but beneficial for our Great Republic at this critical juncture in our history.

CHAPTER TWENTY-EIGHT

COURT-MARTIAL OR EXCOMMUNICATE THOSE THAT QUESTION CLIMATE CHANGE?

At the 2015 commencement exercise for the United States Coast Guard Academy, President Barack Obama told the graduates this of climate change, "It is a dereliction of duty. Denying it or refusing to deal with it endangers our national security." Later that year, according to a *Boston Globe* report, Cardinal Oscar Rodríguez Maradiaga, allegedly one of Pope Francis's closest advisors in The Vatican, said, "The ideology surrounding environmental issues is too tied to a capitalism that doesn't want to stop ruining the environment because they don't want to give up their profits."

These two statements from such disparate world quarters are frightening in their implications. A military member who now dares to question climate change has committed an offense under Article 92 of the Uniform Code of Military Justice punishable by up to two years imprisonment and a dishonorable discharge. And, a Roman Catholic who questions it is potentially guilty of the sins of envy or greed.

Such militancy from a sitting president and a powerful cardinal is not only offensive and misleading, but it does not bode well for the immediate security of the United States or the spiritual health of the Church. This crazy, frenetic intemperance was taken to a new level in 2016, when sitting United States Attorneys from albeit liberal enclaves actually considered filing *criminal* charges against those they label "Climate Deniers."

First, it is far from settled science as to whether or not man is capable of significantly impacting the Earth's cyclical warming and cooling. Ask any supporter of the climate change theory the following question: "Why do the coolest and hottest periods in recorded history occurred *prior* to the Industrial Revolution?" Such a question is most often met with a smirk, raised eyebrow or anger, never a logical answer. Confront progressives with facts and they simply raise their voice. But when this president and this cardinal, and others within the seats of power make ad hominem attacks and threats against those who honestly and correctly challenge them on this point of fact it is plainly hateful and pusillanimous. It is also dangerous because it squelches honest pursuits of the truth.

There is simply not enough space here to debate the facts underpinning whether man can impact God's Universe to the degree claimed by the environmental movement (there is simply not enough space here to do so and such is not the issue) it is the solipsistic nature of such claims that is most disconcerting. Instead of a God-centric view, environmentalists support modernity's "man-centric" worldview in which it is assumed that man, not God, is the ultimate purveyor of truth and rational thought. This extends to their view of Natural Law, of which they are similarly dismissive. For Obama and Maradiaga, modernity holds sway over eternal truths.

The Catholic Church loses much of its majesty and authority when its senior leaders dabble in contentious politics such as this. Even in seeming great human struggles such as the Spanish Civil War, true priestly wisdom, not passion, guides souls. This was the beautiful message of Saint Josemaría Escrivá, who founded *Opus Dei* during that contentious era. One can find no such beauty, peace or wisdom in the words of Cardinal Maradiaga, only divisive anger and, probably, woeful scientific ignorance.

For a President of the United States, in a world where radical Islamists are beheading and crucifying children and killing by the score Americans *in* America; trying to obtain nuclear armaments; and threatening the homeland with lone-wolf attacks, to focus on climate change as a priority national security issue is troubling at best. But, nothing that Barack Obama did should surprise rational thinkers. Maradiaga and Obama share a common faith in the errant voices of Modernity, as reflected in the words and actions the environmental movement and its spiritual cousins liberation theology and socialism.

Both America and the Catholic Church need leaders that focus on promoting virtues and teaching universal truths. Currying favor with the faces and beliefs of modernity is dancing with the devil. At the end of the dance, the devil is only interested in stealing both virtue and the truth. We no longer question Obama's choice of a dance partner, as he has made that abundantly clear by word and deed. We do, however, expect better of Vatican City.

CHAPTER TWENTY-NINE

GOD AND MAN IN THESE UNITED STATES

WITH
JOHN TAYLOR

Those faithful to the Constitution have been teetering on the edge of despair for the past eight years. With hope and strength, we can retain our soul and, in turn, regain our wits. Put simply, too many have turned the notion of God-Country-Man on its head. Man now wants to be his own god and we are suffering the worse for it. A portrait of this problem is the case of Bruce Jenner.

The winner of the Decathlon in the 1976 Olympic Games, Jenner was a household name who visage graced the cover of *Time* Magazine and boxes of Wheaties. Fast-forward four decades and we find a man unable to gracefully cope with relative anonymity. Bruce decided he was not happy being a man as God created him. So, he spends fortunes on surgery and other therapy, throws on a wig, and declares he is a woman.

In a rational society, guided by virtues handed down from our Creator through generations, his case may have made a sad column on the back pages of the sports section of newspapers.

In modern America, Jenner is given an ESPY award as the Courageous Athlete of the Year. Ignoring the obvious questions of whether Jenner is still an athlete and why his personal decision was more courageous than a host of other athletes exhibiting true courage this past year, we simply posit the following.

What if Michael Jordan, arguably the greatest basketball player of all time, decides to cut off one leg and declare himself a flamingo? Would ESPN[1] give Michael an award? And if not, why not? Would not his personal decision to defy God's plan be just as "courageous" as Jenner's? There is no moral distinction between the two cases. And, the fact that a larger minority of people undergo a so-called transgender sex change than do those becoming denying God to become a flamingo ought to make Michael Jordan's hypothetical act being even more courageous.

But, such logic cannot be tolerated in our Orwellian world. In this brave new age, an athlete, in this case Brett Favre, who dared not applaud vociferously enough at the ESPY award show, is made the villain by the Progressive media. This smacks of North Korea's rule under their Dear Leader.

On a humorous side, it is akin to the following scene in *Blazing Saddles* where Mel Brooks' character, Governor Petomane, is angered for the same reason.

Governor William J. Le Petomane: [pointing to a member of his cabinet] I didn't get a "harrumph" out of that guy!

Hedley Lamarr: Give the Governor harrumph!

Politician: Harrumph!

Brett Favre obviously didn't harrumph Jenner's "courage" with enough vigor to please the thought police. Never mind that Johnny Unitas, or any man of his generation, would have gotten up and walked out. Now people are not allowed to hold a differing moral position on any matter that has received Hollywood's imprimatur. Now, we have the likes of San Francisco 49ers quarterback Colin Kaepernick failing to stand for the National Anthem because he thinks he has been discriminated against due to his race. Many would wish to be discriminated against like he has been, earning millions of dollars a season for playing football!

By way of contrast to Kaepernick (whose image I will never portray), check out Sergeant Zachary Stinson, USMC, using his arms to stand in his wheelchair for the playing of the "Star-Spangled Banner:

CHAPTER THIRTY

OBAMA, PUTIN AND THE UKRAINE - THE LOST HONOR OF THE AMERICAN PRESIDENCY

From an American perspective, the situation simmering in The Crimea and Eastern Ukraine is interesting for an obvious number of geopolitical reasons. It bears an eerie likeness to the Russian intervention into Georgia in 2008 and, to a lesser extent, an historical parallel to Germany's "concern" for the Sudeten Deutsch in 1938. In addition to all the direct implications for Ukrainians' freedom, there are significant other second and third order effects that a twenty-first century Crimean War might incur. But, on a personal and national political level, the matter has squeezed the pus to a head of the boil so illustrative of Barack Obama's character.

As a fourth-generation combat veteran and retired military officer, I never thought that I would root or cheer any foreign opponent of the President of these United States. For the reasons, set forth below, I could not wait for Vladimir Putin to figuratively break his leg off up Obama's hindquarters. Most concern a deep lack of values or moral compass of behalf of the

American president. This overlooked cultural difference is what concerns Russians in general and Putin specifically.

First and foremost, Obama forced the military to give supernumerary "protected-class status" to homosexuals and, now "transgenders" (that innocuous sounding bit of newspeak that describes those that in a more civilized and virtuous era who were committed to a loony bin). Not only was this in defiance of the personal religious convictions of the majority of military personnel, but also this sole cultural difference between Russians and the "progressive" West is at the root of the current problem in the Crimea.

The EU and United States of the Cold War were exemplified by the likes of Konrad Adenauer and Ronald Reagan. These were folks that had their moral compass in synchronization with a strong Judeo-Christian polestar. They would not recognize or acknowledge the radical and aggressive homosexual lobby and its fruits. Most in the West are ignorant of this reality or are so cowed by the coercively politically correct that they are afraid to voice this truth.

So, the brewing new "Cold War" is not one between capitalism and communism, but rather between progressivism that lacks a moral compass and an old school Russian Rodina orthodoxy that refutes such an absence of moral integrity and spirituality. Our friend, Ethicist, Author and Attorney, Alexandre Havard writes of this in his lovely 2016 autobiography *My Russian Way*. Mother Russia, the Rodina, despite seven decades under the yoke of Lenin and Stalinist Communism, has remained deeply and stoically mystical.

As I recently commented to a fellow officer at one of our service academies, "What prevents one from marrying a goat? For if you have already ceded the issue of marriage to a matter of personal choice, then how can you dare judge one's choice to marry that goat?" The Russians see this as a serious assault on their ingrained moral culture. When the EU threatens to expand its ever-aggressive political correctness to the Ukraine and when Hillary Clinton, that paradigm of virtue, compares Vladmir Putin to Adolf Hitler, one can hardly blame them. Strangely, the coercive central government is now NATO, and Russia *appears* to be the one clamoring for religious and culture freedom.

On top of this, by his complete disregard for our Constitution and the rule of law, Barack Obama far exceeded the petty criminal acts of Richard Nixon. The bill of particulars of a prospective indictment would be too wordy to cite here. In shorthand it would contain: myriad Executive Orders circumventing Congressional authority; criminal misuse of the IRS to target political opponents; willful violation of the Fourth Amendment rights of nearly every American by domestic spy programs; and, conspiring with radical Islamic groups in order to undermine the Judeo-Christian heritage and common law of our republic.

By widening and deepening the gap between the races in direct contravention to his campaign rhetoric to heal and mend racial discord, Obama singularly did more than any president in history to foment racial discord. Despite the fact that Barack Obama is genetically more white and Asian than Black, he consistently identified issues based on their visceral appeal to black racial animosity. From his "if I had a son" comments after the Trayvon Martin shooting to his recent review and awarding of the Medal of Honor to veterans of past wars solely because of their skin color (ignoring similarly situated white combat heroes like Dick Winters or Chesty Puller who had their Medal of Honor recommendations downgraded for petty, bureaucratic reasons), this fellow never missed an opportunity to stir the tired stew of racial hatred and pettiness.

This man-child systemically removed warriors from the ranks of general and flag officers solely on their perceived lack of political loyalty; and, cut defense funding to pre-WWII levels. Moreover, while he wantonly killed hundreds, if not thousands, of noncombatants as collateral damage to his drone strikes, he sanctioned and abided by the courts-martial of young warriors like Army Lieutenant Clint Lorance for the few civilian deaths they may have caused based on decision made in the heat of battle. This is the height of arrogance and the depths of poor leadership. His actions did more to damage our Republic than any former foreign enemy of the Cold War could have dreamed of doing. By clear and convincing evidence, Barack Obama is a rabid anti-American who never would have been given a security clearance if subjected to an objective and impartial single scope background investigation. And Americans trusted him not once, but twice (if one believes the results of the 2012 elections were not skewed by fraud) with the keys to our worldly kingdom.

Instead of being a virtuous and magnanimous leader that promotes courage, self-control, justice, and competency in our government, he is small-minded and selfish. Barack Obama's moral compass must be ranked lowest amongst significant world leaders (only slightly higher than the heads of Iran and North Korea). Twice, mostly good-natured Americans put their trust into someone worse than a novice. "Putin is playing chess and I think we are playing marbles," said House Intelligence Committee Chairman Mike Rogers a while back. But, Obama was something more dangerous than a novice. Each passing day of his administration showed him to be nothing less than a *Manchurian Candidate* bent on destroying our culture and economy in order to create equality as he sees it. Winston Churchill once quipped, "The greatest vice of capitalism is the unequal sharing of blessings, while the great greatest virtue of socialism is the equal sharing of miseries." Again, was it any wonder that Obama's first act as president was to ungraciously return a bust of Churchill to the United Kingdom?

Without any rancor or ill will to the people of the Ukraine, I waited with a bit of glee and *Schadenfreude* for Putin to again publicly thumb his nose at our pusillanimous president. Afterward, I prayed that our Congress initiates impeachment proceedings against this dangerous child and our Nation restores its obeisance to the Natural Law and acknowledgement that God's moral order matters to its very survival. Unfortunately, that did not happen. So, the best we can now hope for is that President Trump will damn him by reversing all the ills he foisted on America.

When a deranged veteran with severe PTSD murdered Navy SEAL Chris Kyle, the single most deadly sniper in US history, Obama, he says nothing. When Army Major General Harold Greene, is killed by enemy fire in Afghanistan, the highest-ranking officer killed in the line of duty in that long war. Obama, he says nothing. The list goes on and on. Yet, when a cocaine-snorting pop singer dies, Obama, he orders flags flown at half-mast. He is a despicable, Constitution-hating son of a bitch that, but for certain sections of Title 18, many would gladly have dispatched.

CHAPTER THIRTY-ONE

OUR MILITARY BECOMES ALICE IN WONDERLAND?

The Obama administration and other purveyors of Modernity have hurt the capabilities and esprit de corps of our armed forces far more than Nikita Khrushchev could have ever dreamed of doing back in 1961 when he banged his shoe on the desktop at the UN. First, Obama ordered the military to allow homosexuals, lesbians and cross-dressers to serve openly. His Secretary of the Air Force Secretary Deborah Lee James, in support of the transgender matter, said, "Times change." Asked whether dropping the ban would affect military readiness, she replied, "From my point of view, anyone who is capable of accomplishing the job should be able to serve."[1]

"Times change" is the moral barometer for leading and guiding our republic's Air Force? Secretary Lee is missing the point for a number of reasons. First and foremost, our military should be all about closing with and destroying our Nation's enemies on potential fields of battle, *not* placating the loud and vicious voice of the LGBTQ lobby. Military service is not a right, but a privilege that should be reserved for only the morally and physically fit. As so eloquently stated by Colonel

John W. Ripley, USMC in his testimony before the presidential
commission on homosexuals in the military in 1993,

> *In our present role, the armed forces have moved away from
> the traditional role of fighting and winning, into a more
> bizarre and unintended role as an engine of social change.
> We have become, in effect, a large Petri dish where social
> laboratories and experimenters can create new systems
> or grow new models to test . . . As you know, and as has
> been said here over and over, service in the military is a
> privilege extended only to those who are fit and physically
> able to perform military service. We in the military are very
> discriminatory. We have always been, and it must be so. We
> discriminate between the too weak, the too tall, the too fat,
> the flat-footed, the disease ridden, single parents, morally
> corrupt, drug users, alcoholics, or abusers of any substance;
> we discriminate against the altogether good Americans
> who simply can't be expected to perform at our standards.
> Homosexuals constantly focus on themselves; their so-called
> needs, what they want, their entitlements, their rights; they
> never talk about the good of the unit. It is this constant focus
> on themselves; the inability to subjugate or to subordinate
> their own personal desire for the good of the unit; this is an
> instant indicator of trouble in combat; and frankly, even
> not in combat.*[2]

A true knight of the twentieth century, Colonel Ripley
exemplified such selfless sacrifice and courage in everything he
did. In fact, while fighting through days of exhausting combat,
culminating in his single-handedly emplacing hundreds
of pounds of high explosives to raze the bridge while under

withering enemy fire, this Marine repetitively prayed and chanted, "Jesus, Mary, get me there." His action on that day is considered one of the greatest examples of concentrated valor under fire in the annals of US military history. A mural at the United States Naval Academy depicts that particular battle and act of heroism. While best known for his actions at Dong Ha, for which he was awarded the Navy Cross, our nation's second-highest award for valor, this modern-day knight was also wounded in diverse other battles and was the recipient of the Silver Star, America's third highest award for valor, and two Bronze Stars with *V* for valor.

The media and a coterie of congressional progressives vilified Ripley for his candor back then, yet most Americans – especially those serving in the Armed Forces – agreed with him. They still do. Yet, twenty years later, like a thief in the night (and done *after* his second term election so as to hide his intentions from the public during that close race), the Obama Administration opened the sacred gates of the military to perverts. Not satisfied with simply allowing them to serve, Barack Obama has viciously attempted the forced affirmation of their lifestyles by making warriors attend mandatory gay pride events.

Ripley's predictions about the selfish nature of these groups has been fulfilled in the last few years, as the military now spent most of its energies on such gripping matters as "sexual assault awareness training" and "transgender integration of berthing and latrines." And no one should be surprised that self-absorbed individuals such as Bradley Manning (I refuse to call him "Chelsea" as do his adoring progressive media acolytes, even after Obama pardoned him in the eleventh hour) would violate their non-disclosure agreements and oaths not to divulge sensitive top-secret information. There was a reason why these types were non-selected for service. It is a wonder Manning could have survived any serious single-scope background investigation (SSBI) that is supposed to be a precursor and gatekeeper to such a high level of security clearance.

Sexual conduct, preference or activity should be subordinated to service. While I have served with some men that I highly suspected were indifferent to women, those men just did their duty and would never have felt the need to openly proclaim their differences or seek the affirmation of others. In other words, Don't Ask, Don't Tell (DADT) worked. But, that was not enough for the *rabid* LGBTQ crowd, for whom, like Obama, everything appears to be about self rather than mission. The Administration unnecessarily set America on a collision course between those possessing deeply held religious beliefs concerning what constitutes deviant behavior and those wishing to "celebrate" their sexual differences. For that, it should be ashamed. But, shame requires an acknowledgement of a higher deity and a natural law. This Administration acknowledges neither.

Drifting about without acknowledging the natural law by which man should govern his actions raises the question of what comes next: bestiality, pedophilia or "marrying" an inanimate object and proclaiming that thing is one's husband or wife? According to a Secretary James' progressive "logic" all that matters is the desire and ability of an individual to serve. So, how could she rightly discriminate against any of the above?

Colonel Ripley knew better, and his predictions have come to fruition. Plunging budgets, increased male on male sexual assaults and, now, forced integration of cross-dressing sad human beings like Bradley Manning are issues that taking up the majority of our commanders' time. And where are the voices of our general and flag officers in these matters? In their heart of hearts, when they look at themselves in the mirror at night, do they see the reflection of a John W. Ripley or the hollow shadow of their own cowardice slouching toward their next promotion?

We have witnessed, firsthand, the muzzling of free and open debate in the military on this topic, but it is one that is not dead yet: not by a long shot. And it is still possible for a courageous future Commander-in-Chief to put this awful genie back into the bottle. Colonel Ripley died on November 1, 2008, All Saints' Day, so he did not have to witness such abominations while still here on this Earth. His grave is hallowed ground at Annapolis. Yet, I am sure that Ripley is in heaven praying for the deliverance of our great Republic and his beloved Marines from such pestilence. Perhaps, the Progressives will try to disinter his grave as they have already done to many heroes of the Confederacy. My great-great grandfather, Captain Burke, fought with Colonel Harry Gilmor's Confederate Raiders in and around Maryland. The Veteran's Administration recently proclaimed by fiat that one is no longer allowed to mark such a veteran's grave with a Confederate battle flag. It might offend someone. But, you see, like Stalin and Hitler, only socialists are allowed to be offended. God help the poor bastard that tries to keep me from planting a Confederate battle flag on my ancestors' graves.

CHAPTER THIRTY-TWO

COLOR ME GONE! VIRTUE IN AMERICA AND CECIL THE LION

America awoke that morning to read banner headlines concerning world outrage that an American bow hunter killed a male lion in Zimbabwe. Jimmy Kimmel weighed in on the Cecil the Lion, and according to *Hollywood Reporter*, "choking up a little as he made clear his disgust and likened the present hatred of hunter Walter Palmer to the public's feeling towards Bill Cosby." Throughout my adult life, from Iraq and Afghanistan to walking a police beat in the public housing projects of Baltimore, I have hunted criminals, enemies, and animals. I know a bit about human suffering and have witnessed courage and virtue amongst many colleagues in the face of true adversity. So, at first, I was tempted to laugh aloud at how emasculated American males have become, crying over a dead lion. What would John Wayne or Gary Cooper think?

Then a more ominous issue peeked through this specious umbrage. Hundreds of young people are murdered every year in our major cities; two videos have recently surfaced showing government-funded Planned Parenthood doctors casually discussing infanticide in order to sell body parts, and, our president, when not congratulating homosexual athletes and transvestites, just inked a deal giving nuclear arms to crazed Islamists in Iran. And the best that the America public can muster is outrage over a clean, lawful and valiant stalking and killing of a wild animal by Dr. Palmer, a Minnesota dentist and bow hunter? If there was any uncertainty that we have lost our moral compass, this brouhaha should put a stake through the heart of that doubt.

Young men growing up in better days had hunters like Daniel Boone, Simon Kenton, or latter-day warriors like Elmer Keith and Frederick Selous, to emulate and venerate. Of Revolutionary War fame, Tennessee's fierce Overmountain Men were all hunters and scouts, progenitors of real twentieth century American heroes like Alvin York (a hunter too) and many members of the combat arms. Anyone familiar with the art of hunting recognizes bow hunters as the sine qua non of the hunting community, especially those who hunt dangerous game with a bow. The nation's degradation from one whose celebrities once aspired to such manly virtues to one where television hosts weep over the wild beasts is troubling. Truly, John Wayne, Jimmy Stewart, Clark Gable, and Gary Cooper, men of honor and stout deed, must be rolling in their graves.

Our armed forces, specifically the ones at the tip of the spear, the Special Forces, Rangers, infantry, and SEALs, draw heavily from those raised in the rural hunting world where self-reliance, toughness and bravery in the face of charging animals are praiseworthy character traits. Now, a hunter, who paid his license fees and stalked a male lion in the bush, as did King David, has to go into hiding due to the calumny heaped upon him by sissies like Jimmie Kimmel. What message does this send to America's young men?

But, the very fact that more of the world weeps over a dead lion than they seem to for their fellow humans, especially our most innocent infants, is the most troubling aspect of this story. Whether the byproduct of Disney fantasy movies or hardcore animal rights groups that anthropomorphize beasts or, worse, place concern for animals over their fellow man; the fact that a taxpaying hunter and dentist is now vilified for killing a lion is the definition of a society gone mad.

Peggy Noonan once commented, "What were once vices are now government-sponsored activities." Gambling, abortion, and homosexuality are now celebrated. Take a look at a recent invitation from the Command General of Fort Benning, Georgia: the place where we forge America's Infantryman and Armor Forces:

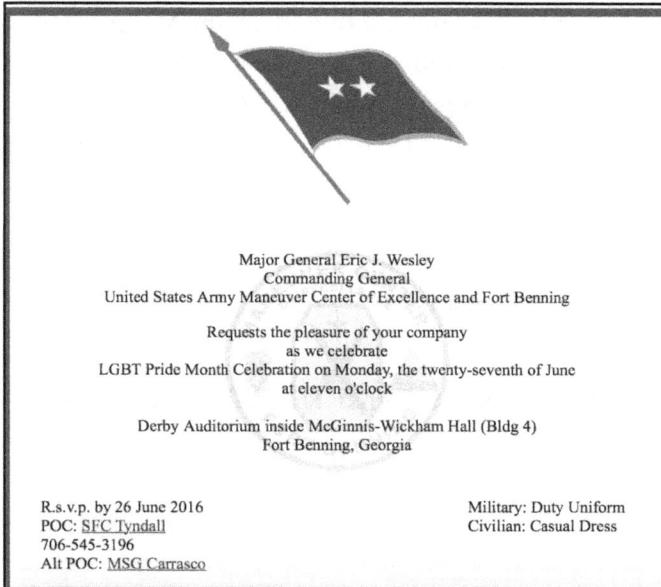

Major General Eric J. Wesley
Commanding General
United States Army Maneuver Center of Excellence and Fort Benning

Requests the pleasure of your company
as we celebrate
LGBT Pride Month Celebration on Monday, the twenty-seventh of June
at eleven o'clock

Derby Auditorium inside McGinnis-Wickham Hall (Bldg 4)
Fort Benning, Georgia

R.s.v.p. by 26 June 2016   Military: Duty Uniform
POC: SFC Tyndall   Civilian: Casual Dress
706-545-3196
Alt POC: MSG Carrasco

If this does not make you want to puke, we are done.

CHAPTER THIRTY-THREE

OBAMA'S COGNITIVE DISSONANCE

The first President of the United States I was old enough to vote for was Ronald Wilson Reagan in 1980. But, that did not prevent me from diligently reading every issue of *National Review* and watching William F. Buckley Jr.'s terrific television show *Firing Line*. Buckley's interview with socialist/agnostic turned Roman Catholic Malcolm Muggeridge on the episode "How One Finds Faith" is classical Liberalism's answer to Modernity's Progressive nihilism. With such a perspective at the time I thought no President in my lifetime would ever be as bad as Jimmy Carter. How wrong 36 years of adult life and 8 years of Obama's reign have made me.

Two of his most glaringly displays of woeful ignorance are on the following topics:

BLACK LIVES MATTER AND THE DALLAS/BATON ROUGE MURDERS

Obama reflexively saw everything through the lens of race, this despite the fact that his most prominent genetic code is Caucasian (his mother was all-white; his father was not all-African). When domestic terror groups like Black Lives Matter cause the murder of innocent police officers throughout the nation, Obama blamed the NRA and so-called white privilege. Never mind that every rational analysis of police shootings shows (a) proportionally police shoot more white suspects than black; and, (b) the suspects themselves are the authors of their own misfortune. Instead of placing the moral onus on those responsible, the urban blacks committing atrocious acts of violence against their own communities, Obama spoke of gun violence as if that were a thing capable of possessing specific or general intent: it isn't. Gun violence can be good or bad. I have personally used gun violence to stop an armed robber and have facilitated the use of gun violence against terrorists in Iraq, Afghanistan, and elsewhere.

As writer John Gibbs so presciently stated in his article "How Obama Left Us More Racially Divided Than Ever" appearing on *TheFederalist.com*,

> *I believe that when President Obama thinks of America, more so than a place of hope or opportunity, he thinks of a place where racist white Christian fundamentalists came here from Europe, committed genocide against Native Americans, enslaved and segregated black people, denied women, gays, and other minorities their rights, and used capitalism and a rigged legal system to oppress poor people for centuries. He also believes this is still continuing today.*

Obama is a man who had every opportunity to bring America's races closer to each other, to see each other as fellow citizens rather than hyphenated antagonists. He, along with Eric Holder and Loretta Lynch, perpetuated that with the whole black-white dialogue and then with LGBT nonsense.

Prayerfully, the Trump/Spence White House will start mending our Country and supporting our peace officers.

COMBATING TERRORISM

When Obama spoke about terrorism, his warped vision and, sadly, the vision of too many technocrats in the EU, was that Globalism would defeat terrorism. Yes, I suppose it would in the same manner National Socialism or Stalin's Communism stifled dissent! Globalism is the root cause of terrorism, as are borders that have become so porous as to allow all sorts of honor-ritual-death cultures to pour into Christendom. Rather, as the truism so rightly quoted by poet Robert Frost, "Good fences make good neighbors." When my wife and I travel to Europe, we want to see Germans in Germany, Italians in Italy and so on. Obama's seeming worldview where everyone looks the same, dresses the same and acts the same is a nightmarish worldview of the *Star Trek* generation: the Sixties radicals and hippies. Hillary Clinton and Barack Obama are nothing more than elite patchouli-smelling hippies. It is time for America to bury them with their sick dreams and start making our Republic great again!

CHAPTER THIRTY-FOUR

THOUGHTS ON BEING A SERVANT LEADER

Y ou have to have confidence in your commanders and must give them authority. If they make a mistake out of malice you punish them and if they make a mistake out of ignorance, you actually reward them because you want people to continue to have flexibility and creativity. Desire risk taking in commanders who are not afraid of opportunities — Machiavelli, *The Discourses On Livy*.

Real men, real *leaders* love and trust their subordinates because they have trained so well as to ensure each man possesses the Cardinal Virtues of (1) Moral Courage; (2) Competency; (3) Self-Control; and (4) a real sense of Justice, designed to give each man his due and latitude to exercise discretion.

The current misunderstanding of the law, ethics, and tactics amongst many members of the judiciary, political class, and leadership, including within our law enforcement and military commands, has resulted in good guys being killed or unduly exposed to criminal liability from deadly force encounters. The law is clear and firm on the use of force, but in recent years, a politically driven cloud has obscured the clarity of such law and reason. Consequently, in some circumstances *career* survival has taken the place of *street* survival. And often the confusion originates with leadership. Therefore, leadership *must* be servant in its nature: service to the populace and to subordinates.

US Marine Sergeant Jasen Wrubel dragged his foot behind him while patrolling with his squad on April 2, 2009 in Now Zad, Afghanistan. Sergeant Wrubel dragged his feet to create a safe path for his fellow Marines to follow safely in single file. Taliban fighters had buried IEDs throughout the city to kill US forces on patrol.

(Photo by John Moore/Getty Images)

While, due to our divers circumstances and stations in life, we cannot all be a Sergeant Wrubel, literally dragging our feet through mine fields to protect our brothers. But, figuratively, we can strive for such a servant-leader lifestyle in our daily lives. Now, perhaps as no other time in our Republic's history, it is time for men and women of courage to stand up and be counted. While it has become so trite as to be a truism, "All it takes for evil to triumph is for good men to do and say nothing" is emphatically important in the dawn of the twenty-first century. We were one election away from waving goodbye to the freedoms we knew as children, which surely would have happened if Clinton were elected. I will not go silently into the night and I trust and pray that I am not alone.

CHAPTER THIRTY-FIVE

FIXING THE MILITARY'S
(AND SOCIETY'S) MORAL COMPASS

Alexandre Havard[1] writes in *Virtuous Leadership* on the importance and relevance of the cardinal virtues–prudence, fortitude (or **courage**), temperance (or **self-control**) and **justice**–to both leaders and organizations. Any person or group that lacks in one or more of these core character traits is doomed to failure. As William Penn, the founder and namesake of Pennsylvania said,

> *Governments, like clocks, go from the motion men give them; and as governments are made and moved by men, so by them they are ruined too ... Let men be good and the government cannot be bad ... But if men be bad, let the government be never so good, they will endeavor to warp and spoil it to their turn*[2]

Likewise, our military and society depends on good people to lead and man it. Historically, it has consistently embraced the cardinal virtues to better ensure a spirit of selfless sacrifice and service amongst its members. Herodotus's commentary on the duties of the ancient Persians, "to ride well, shoot straight, and speak the truth,"[3] recognizes that there are absolute truths and an internal moral compass that warriors should follow. We have failed a generation of young men, turning too many of them into emasculated, effeminate pussies who are too afraid to shoot a rifle or speak the truth. Hell, they can't even summon the moral courage to acknowledge there are such things as universal truths or the natural law!

These beliefs have formed the cornerstone of our military's ethos. It is now under subtle attack by those that decry such beliefs as antiquated or even unconstitutional. Such efforts must be soundly repulsed, as military leaders' moral compasses must be immune to quaint notions of modernity that recognize no fundamental truths.

For years, living by the cardinal virtues has inoculated the military from self-absorbed, licentious behaviors such as one routinely observes in Hollywood and professional sports leagues. America's modern military culture has fairly consistently remained above the fray of partisan politics and the gutter of licentiousness. Unfortunately, there are those trying to change that very culture by marginalizing the voices of virtue within our force.

If the armed forces of the United States are to remain a dominant player in geopolitics as well as a guardian of our populace, it must not proceed under the false belief that aspiring to live virtuously is somehow an antiquated and irrelevant modality for a postmodern world. The first obstacle often thrown out by those objecting to infusing virtue's lessons into policy is that doing so somehow violates the Constitution of the United State's First Amendment's Establishment Clause, which proscribes a formal church-state relationship.

Such an objection is a canard that is predicated on ignorance of history and the law. Historically, discussions of the cardinal virtues can be found not only in all of the world's major religions, but also in classical literature and philosophy. Legally, those that rail against any open religious activity in the military, such as the presence of a Chaplains' Corps, seem to ignore the Free Exercise Clause of that very same constitutional amendment. Sadly, these voices have found traction of late within the Executive Branch.[4]

THE CARDINAL VIRTUES

PRUDENCE OR COMPETENCY

A well-used proverb states that one rarely finds an old head head on young shoulders.. Hence, this virtue, like all the others, must be taught and learned. Aristotle defined prudence as recta ratio agibilium, meaning "right reason applied to practice." In the military, this is reflected in a commander who has mastered fundamental tasks so well that in the fog of war these are enabling rather than distracting. At a purely tactical level, it is that Visit Board Search and Seizure (VBSS) team member so intimate with his weapon systems that he can focus on potential threats not on whether his weapon's selector switch is on safe or fire.

When a leader consistently makes wrong decisions – or makes rash decisions, right or wrong – then that individual is imprudent. Due to the complexity of the modern battlefield, it is easy to err in this fashion. Accordingly, competent leaders seek the counsel of others and quickly learn to delegate responsibilities and authorities to trusted subordinates. They also encourage freethinking amongst their staff. Those assigned to a dysfunctional staff, where the commander browbeats those who disagree, will instantly recognize this lack of virtue in their boss. "Don't be the nail that stick above the surface," is the unspoken advice in such commands. Sadly, courageous subordinates are often crushed; while sycophants, or those who simply remain silent, get promoted.

Prudence or competency is the result of practice. But, it also may require personal humility. Disregarding the advice or warnings of others whose judgment does not coincide with one's own may be a sign of imprudence. It is possible that the commander is right and his staff wrong; but the opposite may be true, especially if the commander is consistently disagreeing with those whose demonstrated judgment is sound. Absent a moral barometer, either derived from Natural Law or the Ten Commandments, there is no measure of right reason. Accordingly, bad commanders will simply bully others to get their way. That is why assaults upon the military's seemingly archaic moral code are so intrinsically dangerous. For he who believes in everything believes nothing and, consequently, lacks a compass by which to steer a true and straight course.

JUSTICE

Prudence or competency is the internal focus of one's intellectual abilities: the application of right reason to a given problem. Justice is more outwardly focused. It is that trait which seeks to give everyone his or her rightful due. This requires much more than simply abiding by the rules set forth in the Uniform Code of Military Justice (UCMJ) or General Orders. While maintaining discipline in the Armed Forces is very important to the orderly conduct of military operations, and most people desire and expect malefactors to be brought to justice, the *virtue* of Justice is much greater than the sum of what is set forth in those rules and procedures. Good commanders utilize Justice as a positive motivator on the path toward a humble and magnanimous career for themselves and their subordinates.

Members of a successful military command are more concerned with respecting the rights of others and giving them proper credit where credit is due. It was said of Field Marshal William Slim, Commander of the China-Burma-India Theater of Operations in World War II, that he never said *I* rarely said, *We*, and always said *You*.[1] Sam Damon, the protagonist in Anton Myer's brilliant novel *Once an Eagle*, further exemplifies such a person. Damon is a professional warrior who puts duty, honor, and the men he commands above self-interest. He justly earns his promotions. The book's antagonist, Courtney Massengale, is an unjust, self-absorbed bully who advances by political scheming and trampling upon subordinates and contemporaries. *Once an Eagle* should be mandatory reading for all officers and noncommissioned officers. The Commanding General at Fort Benning cited in the previous chapter either did not read it or forgot its enduring truths.

Justice also requires an acknowledgement and obeisance to the natural law or divinely inspired law. Absent such a framework, we are left with simply the subordinate laws and whims of man. We would be well served to remember that Adolf Hitler did nothing *illegal* under the laws of the Third Reich. The reason that Hitler's acts were so unspeakable is that they contravened divine or natural law. A just leader respects both the natural rights of others (to be secure in life and limb, their obligations to family and associates, fundamental property rights, and to practice one's religion and hold sacred beliefs) and the legal rights of others (command authorities, the UCMJ, personal contract rights, and other rights and entitlements found under the law). Should legal rights ever come into conflict with natural rights, however, the latter take precedence. Hence, a warrior has both a right and obligation to disobey clearly unlawful, unethical or unconstitutional orders. Without an underlying concept of right or wrong – what is Justice – how would a service member ever be able to discern this?

COURAGE

One may assume that anyone donning the uniform of the armed forces has *physical* courage. However, what is being discussed here is an overarching *moral* courage. A person could be physically courageous enough to charge a machinegun nest, but still be a moral coward in other important leadership capacities. Moral courage, or fortitude, is that rock-steady virtue that seeks to elevate others above self. Competency and Justice are the virtues by which we decide what *ought* to be done. Courage provides us the will and strength to do so, even in the face of obstacles. For day-to-day life, it is the constant practice of seeking and speaking the truth in the face of adversity or peer pressure to do otherwise. It is what gives that subordinate staff officer the strength to raise a hand during a command briefing and disagree with a politically expedient, but morally wrong or unjust, course of action.

Courage may require one to speak out against: voguish but evil spirits of the times; impure conduct or trends; and, the common tendency to seek the path of least resistance. It also requires one to speak the truth even if doing so may be personally painful: "For if we sin willfully after that we have received the knowledge of the truth, there remaineth no more sacrifice for sins" (Hebrews 10:26).

The New Testament also speaks to those who "are willingly ignorant."[2] The meaning is the same. It is one thing to be unaware of the truth; it is altogether different when people know what is true, yet ignore it out of cowardice or political expediency. By a casual reading of today's headlines, it appears to all but the naïve or complicit that many of our senior military leaders failed under Obama to stand up for what they must, in their hearts, have known to be right and just. This is likely for want of courage.

SELF-CONTROL OR TEMPERANCE

Epistemologically, self-control or temperance demands control of one's animal desire for pleasure. We wring our hands and wonder why so many of our warriors commit acts of sexual assault; and, how come so many flag officers commit other diverse acts of moral turpitude. Often, these acts are a failure to moderate desires in the face of temptation. Self-control is that virtue which attempts to overcome the human condition that best stated as "The spirit indeed is willing, but the flesh is weak." But, if we have institutionally disavowed the notion that there are fundamental rights and wrongs, is it any wonder we are in this quandary?

However, self-control is much more than just tempering base sexual desires. In the realm of virtuous leaders, self-control might mean that: choleric personalities restrain their tempers; impatient persons exercise listening skills; tardiness is replaced by timeliness; or, phlegmatic persons make an effort to be more outgoing. "Everything that grows begins small. It is by constant and progressive feeding that it gradually grows big"[3] This notion applies to seeding and growing virtue in organizations and individual lives. Taking such seemingly small steps can gradually build a command imbued with a sense of unit humility. It can truly help transform an organization from a dour, miserable workplace to a magnanimous command where people are excited and proud to serve.

Magnanimity is an underutilized and not frequently understood word. It is the loftiness of spirit enabling one to bear trouble calmly, to disdain meanness and pettiness, and to display a noble generosity. It is the essence of chivalry. A magnanimous person is the opposite of a pusillanimous or small-minded person. Every military leader should strive to foster an environment where magnanimity flourishes. Absent a deep understanding and practice of the cardinal virtues, however, such a goal is futile because the leader lacks the inherent capacity to foster unit humility and magnanimity.

WORDS OF CAUTION

The dangers for the military not acknowledging and living pursuant to the Cardinal Virtues should be obvious. But, when one considers how to boil a frog,[4] the pitfalls may not be as obvious as they once recently might have been. Just consider the myriad "hot button" issues, critical to the continued integrity and strength of our military, which have now all but been placed "off limits" by senior leaders who seem more concerned with keeping their stars than speaking or hearing the truth. For example, any rational discussion concerning these topics – (1) the possibility that core tenets of Sharia law are incompatible with a Constitutional Republican form of governance that respects religious freedoms; (2) forced *affirmation,* vice *acceptance* of homosexual conduct within our forces; and (3) the inclusion of females into units routinely expected to be engaged in close quarters combat (CQB) missions – has been effectively quashed in today's military. This is true, despite the fact that a majority of those serving have principled questions about each of these topics.

But anyone that questions the wisdom of such policies is, at best, quickly marginalized. Truth, or at least rational attempts to discern the truth, has been labeled as "Hate Speech." In some instances, as in the case of Army Lieutenant Colonel Matthew Dooley whose career was *crushed* by the Chairman of the Joint Chiefs of Staff for daring to raise the aforementioned Sharia issue, otherwise stellar careers are ruined for not toeing the party line. We should do well to heed the words of Isaiah: "Woe to you that call evil good, and good evil: that put darkness for light, and light for darkness: that put bitter for sweet, and sweet for bitter."[5]

While it is imperative, as General of the Army Douglas MacArthur tested during the Korean War, that the military remain subordinate to its civilian masters in matters of policy and strategy; it must nevertheless vigorously resist attempts to dilute its core values by means of crass political bullying. Moreover, if there are rational and moral concerns about any policy or course of action, voices expressing such concerns should be encouraged rather than quelled or shunned. Sadly and dangerously, this does not appear to be happening in today's military.

Trends to muzzle the virtuous voices in the military must be reversed if our Navy, Marine Corps, Air Force, Army, and Coast Guard are to remain morally fit and strong. The silence of the admirals and generals has been deafening in this regard. The Obama's administration's grand experiment to radically transform America has caused serious erosions in our military's capability and discipline; yet, we heard crickets instead of voices of truth and moral incorruptibility from our flag officers.

Consequently, we now have a military that appears more concerned with providing benefits to random sexual partners or forcing the square peg of "gender"[6] equality into the round hole of readiness.

No objectively honest person should be surprised that an overwhelming majority of female candidates simply can't make it through physically demanding courses such as the Army's Ranger School, Marine Infantry Officers Course, Basic Underwater Demolition School (SEAL-BUDS) and Special Forces Qualification Course. By not accepting the fact that "war is hard" and close-quarters combat is necessarily a realm for masculine males, the military scrambles to change the standards to ensure "sex" equality occurs despite costs to our readiness.[7]

When it comes to matters of national defense, specious beliefs in the *physical* equality of the sexes should not trump the harsh reality of the battlefield. There is a reason there are no female athletes in the National Football League (or any other professional sports league): men are better suited to such physical conflict. All the political correct thought and indoctrination in the world can't change this fact of Nature and God's design. If we allow courts or policy makers not anchored by virtues to challenge this immutable truth, we will end up not only with boring sports contests but also a less effective combat force. But, first, we must acknowledge there are immutable facts and truths. Voices of reason and truth, like that expressed by Marine Captain Katie Petronio,[8] are few and far between in this discussion. They appear entirely absent amongst our flag ranks. Hopefully, President Trump will address these concerns and reverse the insane rules imposed by former Secretary of Defense Ash Carter.

Repeating lies loudly and often enough does not make them true. Senior leaders must not simply parrot the opinions of their political masters. Sometimes, the cardinal virtues demand they speak the truth. But, perhaps paralyzed by the fear of losing their stars or not getting a "top block" on that section of their fitness report that demonstrates the proper degree of political correctness, most will remain silent.

Subordinates watch and learn from their leaders. If those leaders go into defilade instead of standing up for what is virtuous, what lessons will be passed down to the next generation? This is not a matter of arguing the value of one combat system over another or the next evolution or revolution of warfare. This is about retaining core virtuous principles that spawn courage, truth and selflessness.

Citizens expect such high standards from its armed forces: it is why a Marine private stands head and shoulders above Occupy Wall Street types or the likes of Bradley Manning (who, sickly, Barack Obama paroled in his last days in office). Service members must forfeit many of their erstwhile civilian idiosyncrasies – faddish haircuts, sleeping late, using illegal drugs, and being couch potatoes – in order to become part of a greater whole. First and foremost, our armed forces should be a corps of moral, disciplined, steely-eyed killers, exemplified by distinguished commanders such as Arleigh Burke, Chesty Puller, and Jim Mattis, that can close with and destroy our Republic's enemies on the seas and fields of battle. Hence, we must never forget to ride, shoot straight and speak the truth: even if doing so ruffles some political feathers. Our warriors and our republic deserve nothing less.

EPILOGUE AND
READING LIST FOR VIRTUOUS
SERVANT LEADERS

"**D**on't try to fool yourself telling me you are weak. You are . . . a coward, which is not the same thing." — *The Way*, Saint Josemaría Escrivá

All Americans who care about preserving and restoring the Republic we loved and once knew need to become twice as industrious as are our enemies. CAIR, Planned Parenthood, Black Lives Matter, Occupy Wall Street, the entire panoply of Leftists and Mohammedan front groups, are not shy about speaking their opinions and forcing their political will upon us. George Soros and his ilk are evil sons of bitches that need to be countered with fire and steel will. Therefore, especially in light of the fact that we are on the side of virtue, we must become twice as active and vocal as the enemy and do not be lazy or weak. If you haven't done so already, join the National Rifle Association, ACT for America, The Federalist Society (especially all lawyers and jurists out there) and support organizations such as the Thomas More Law Center and traditional church groups like Opus Dei and Knights of Columbus for Roman

Catholics. Protestant groups worth joining or following are: James Kennedy/Coral Ridge Ministries, also known as Truth in Action; Family Research Council, headed up by Tony Perkins and Lieutenant General Jerry Boykin, USA (Ret.); Focus on the Family, founded by Dr. James Dobson in the 1970s; and, American Family Association (AFA).

A word of caution here, though, from my Army buddy Ed. B. There are quite a few wolves in sheep's clothing, masquerading under the Christian banner, but liberal/progressive/socialist to the core, so prudent investigation is required before getting associated with what can sometimes be little more than Marxists holding Bibles. These idiots, like their progressive Catholic counterparts, have turned Jesus into a hippie/nice guy rather than the Son of God! Ed also filled me in on a number of outstanding apologetics ministries; among those he especially liked are Answers in Genesis and Ravi Zacharias International Ministries.

Jews in America would be well served by strongly supporting Pro-Israel groups like AIPAC. Moreover, they need to ditch their unholy alliance with the Democratic Party. It is *not* the same Democratic Party of Franklin Roosevelt or even John F. Kennedy. It has veered *hard* left, away from supporting the Zionist cause, and in essence possesses a not-so-closet anti-Semitism that rivals that of *Gentlemen's Agreement*. The State of Israel has long recognized this fact and it just concluded a deal to bring Opus Dei into Israel to lead conventions and expeditions in country.

Politically, first of all, vote! Approximately 50 percent of Americans of voting age do not vote. Your vote counts and by not voting you are passively supporting the likes of She Who Must Not Be Named. Secondly, write *real* snail mail letters to your local, state and federal officials. It matters. Also, write letters to the editor and contribute what you can to candidates that are aligned with the vision of our Republic that our Founders possessed.

It is so very important to read. Turn the television off, except for truly important breaking stories. The rest is mostly pollution. Nothing of real import can fit into a five-second sound bite. It takes effort and time to understand the real issues at hand. The Internet can be either boon or bane, as there are so much half-truths and heresies out there. Also, read history. It truly is a *Distant Mirror* as the title of one of historian Barbara Tuchman's books tells us.

Larry P. Arnn, the president of Hillsdale College, wrote a terrific biography of Sir Winston Churchill. In many places, through Churchill's words and his own insights, Arnn puts nails into the coffin of all the false hopes of Modernity. Here is a snippet:

> *We may think it a gloomy fact that we cannot settle the questions that beckon us to the highest places. Churchill does not. Rather it is "more wonderful than any[thing] that Science can reveal," and it "gives the best hop that all will be well." Even when we deal with forces that are "terrific" and "devastating," our "hearts will ache" and our "lives will be barren" without "a vision above material things." No powerful Science, and no Nazi, can erase that fact or satisfy that need. Resistance to despotism is therefore written in the nature of man.*[1]

Arnn, citing Churchill, writes powerful words here; powerful because they ring true in the heart of any thinking, faithful and contemplative man or woman. That same call to live free stirred the souls of Americans of every generation: Revolutionary patriots; Civil War soldiers on both sides of that conflict; doughboys of the Great War; the soldiers, Marines, sailors and airmen of World War II; those who fought valiantly to keep Communism from infecting South Korea; and those who attempted to keep South Vietnam free (and would have if the American Congress did not defund the war effort after Watergate); and, every warrior who has fought the scourge of despotic Islamism in Somalia, Iraq, and Afghanistan.

Prayerfully, and, remember, Scripture did not say "the gates of Hell will not prevail against the United States," but rather not against "His Church,"[2] we can remain that "shining city on a hill" that John Winthrop wrote of and both John F. Kennedy and Ronald Wilson Reagan strongly believed in. But, without an abiding Faith in God Almighty, the one true God of Israel and Scripture, we *will* perish as that city. While we ought not ever waste energy worrying about matters in the hands of the Almighty, we still must recognize that (1) He gave us free will to chose between good and evil and (2) that he gave this great republic abundant blessings (and "to whom much is given much is expected)." We must not squander this opportunity in history to make the right choices about the future of what has been entrusted to us.

The rapidity at which we have squandered our inheritance of freedom is stark when one takes that moment to step outside the blender and looks at America today versus just fifty short years ago. No one in 1966 would have dreamed that police officers could seize cash from citizens absent probable cause (and that they could keep it without proof of a crime beyond a reasonable doubt!); that we could not freely go to the gates of airports to meet or waive adieu to family and friends coming and going; or, that our religious liberties would be under such attack from the Left. If we continue to surrender our liberty to an all-powerful federal government, our inheritance will vanish and that government will not treat us as a prodigal son but rather as slaves of Pharaoh's Egypt.

The following is just a short list of seemingly diverse and sometimes divergent books and films all possess threads of brilliance in the realm of leading the Judeo-Christian world's fight against the existential threats of both Radical Islam and the Fascism of Modernity (collectivist governance over true freedom). For instance, *Unintended Consequences* provides the best background and history of the importance of personal firearms possession to the preservation of Liberty, but some of its plot devices are sometimes immoral and distracting. I ask the reader to look beyond such error to see the overarching truths Ross's cult classic provides.

BOOKS

Created for Greatness: The Power of Magnanimity by Alexandre Havard

In Defense of Self and Others . . . Issues, Facts & Fallacies -- The Realities of Law Enforcement's Use of Deadly Force (Second Edition) by Urey W. Patrick, John C. Hall

Quartered Safe Out Here by George MacDonald Frasier

Once an Eagle by Anton Myrer

Letters to a Young Catholic by George Weigel

The Great Heresies by Hilaire Belloc

Churchill's Trial by Larry Arnn

The Second World War by Winston S. Churchill
Unintended Consequences by John Ross
Gravity and Grace, Simone Weil

MAGAZINES AND PERIODICALS

Imprimis, Hillsdale College's monthly pamphlet
Proceedings, Naval Institute's monthly magazine

FILMS/DVD

Strategic Leadership lecture of Field Marshal William Slim recorded at the USMC C&GSC in the early 50s

There Be Dragons – Feature movie set in Spanish Civil War

Captains Courageous – 1937 film of a story by Rudyard Kipling

Sergeant York – 1941 film of the story of World War I Medal of Honor recipient

Lonesome Dove – 1989 miniseries starring Robert Duval and Tommy Lee Jones, adapted from the equally good book of the same title by Larry McMurtry

In closing, I want to continuously thank God, the Father, Son, and Holy Ghost (the mystery of the Holy Trinity) and our Blessed Mother for sparing me from the ravages of cancer and forgiving my sins. And, thanks for God's blessing me with outstandingly virtuous parents, John & Eileen Bolgiano, who are now surely with Our Lord in Heaven. And, I offer my love and thanks to my family for their loving me unconditionally and forgiving me for all of my shortcomings as husband and father. My sincerest thanks to my editor, Laura Lisle, at WND. Her efforts made this a much better read: any errors remaining are mine. A debt of gratitude to my military, police and lifetime mentors, Jeff Rosen, Gary Harrell, John C. Hall, Hays Parks, Scott Black, Jack Kaplan, Frank Larkin, Donna Bethel and Robert K. Brown. And my colleagues, Jim Patterson, Morgan Banks, Jason "Doc" Mark, John Taylor,[3] Ed Boyle, Tom Samples, Hawk Holloway, Frank Barile, Bud Johnson, John Nye, Pavel Hubatka, Jose Gordon, Jeff Kirkham, Ed Boyle, Kyle Siegel, Tom Miller, Jay Lovelace, Vince Perez, Jay Santiago (and all my SOCCENT colleagues), Will Norwood, Tom Sheperd and Geoff Wilcox (and too many others left out only by my poor memory) for consistently having my back through thick and thin, good times and bad, and through my personal errors in judgment.

ENDNOTES

PREFACE

1 Hennessy, Brian, "Is 'Religious Extremism' Always a Bad Thing?" *Israel Today*, Monday, August 15, 2016.

2 Sadly, the Progressive Modernists hijacked this beautiful word and, consequently, in the twentieth century it became synonymous with their cheap, humanistic worldview.

3 Ironically, the National Football League and other sports groups have targeted North Carolina for boycott because of that state's law requiring people to use bathrooms based on the sex God gave them.

4 A lifelong friend of my first cousin, Linda Gourash, MD, Laurinda lived a saintly life while alive. Despite being blinded at a young age by a brain hemorrhage, Laurinda possessed a cheerful and caring way about her, always serving others before herself. When I was diagnosed and suffering, my cousin Linda persisted in coming for a visit. Once in my room, she prayed with me to the Blessed Mother and for Laurinda's intercession. Within a month, all the tumors in my chest vanished! The matter is now in the first stages for investigation

for Laurinda's potential veneration or sainthood. This is exciting stuff in this age of disbelief. Sadly, most will ignore it or remain in a state of disbelief. They will believe that Bruce Jenner is a woman, but will not believe that the God that handed Moses the Ten Commandments could possibly be interested in the state of human affairs in the twenty-first century.

5   Forgiveness of my many sins due my living a life of frenetic intemperance . . . I was, at times, a moral coward. But, often I did not know it while living "in the blender" of modernity and striving for rank and position.

6   I shared the same first grade teacher at Baltimore's Cathedral of Mary Our Queen with a much better author, George Weigel. As George so righty wrote in his brilliant book *Letters to a Young Catholic*, Sister Mary Moira could teach a cinder block to read. I was one of them. Even for non-Roman Catholics, I heartily commend Weigel's book. It sparkles with hidden gems from recent and distant past.

7   Silverglate, Harvey, *Three Felonies a Day: How the Feds Target the Innocent*, Encounter Books (2011).

8   Arnn, Larry, *Churchill's Trial*, Nelson Books, Tennessee (2015) at p. 104, quoting Churchill, "Our Duty in India," January 30, 1931, in *His Complete Speeches*, Vol. 5, 2005.

9   1937 study of G.K. Chesterton by Emile Cammaerts, *The Laughing Prophet*.

CHAPTER ONE

1 Within Dar al-Islam itself, all of these people are now being beheaded and crucified.

2 At one point during the battle, the Ottoman leader, Kara Mustafa, personally ordered the execution of 30,000 Christian hostages. ISIS, the Muslim Brotherhood and al Qaeda are nothing new to this cult.

3 *Because They Hate* and *They Must Be Stopped*, published by St. Martin's Press.

CHAPTER FOUR

1 My shift mate in Baltimore Police Department's Southeast District, Vic Gearhart, was suspended in 2016 for calling BLM "thugs." They *are* thugs, but never let truth get in way of strident Leftists: truth loses!

2 "Trump Releases Statement on 'Failed Leadership' of Obama, Hillary", Fox News, August 2, 2016.

CHAPTER SIX

1 It is for these reasons that globalists like Hillary Clinton and Barack Obama truly hate the America our founders so carefully created in the thirteen years between the Declaration of Independence and ratification of the Constitution.

2 Security Clearance paperwork. Many are fearful of speaking the truth because they are more concerned about keeping a clearance (or their rank) than they are about being truly virtuous.

CHAPTER SEVEN

1   Naylor, Sean, *Relentless Strike: The Secret History of Joint Special Operations Command*, Chapter 24, St. Martin's Press (2015).

2   "Law Enforcement Officers Killed & Assaulted", Federal Bureau of Investigation, Criminal Justice Information Services Division, 2015.

3   Eg, Urey Patrick and John C. Hall.

CHAPTER NINE

1   "No Money shall be drawn from the Treasury, but in Consequence of Appropriations made by Law; and a regular Statement and Account of the Receipts and Expenditures of all public Money shall be published from time to time." — US Constitution, Article I, section 9, clause 7.

2   To add insult to this injury, Iran executed an American Intelligence source who was discovered via Hillary Clinton's unsecure email server. Again, "What difference would it had made?" (big dose of sarcasm here).

CHAPTER ELEVEN

1   I have witnessed pleasant, articulate, and thoughtful TSA agents at some airports, but usually they were at smaller airports such as Roswell and Sault Ste. Marie. These agents should be held out as the model of how to treat fellow citizens. Unfortunately, they are the exception rather than the rule.

CHAPTER SIXTEEN

1   In no way is this book the first to address this
    issue. In the scholarly Naval Institute *Proceedings*
    magazine alone, there have been at least two articles
    in the same number of years that address the pros
    and cons of the Millennials' suitability to military
    service. See: Commander Darcie Cunningham's
    "Millennials Bring a New Mentality: Does It
    Fit?" from August 2014 ("The younger generation
    postures to work only the bare minimum number
    of hours required. Additionally, they continuously
    request more time off in the form of early liberty,
    shorter workdays, the ability to go home after
    an office luncheon, and so on. This is aside from
    federal holidays and their 30 days' annual leave.");
    and, Lieutenant Matthew Hipple's "The Millennial
    Debate Presents a False Choice," from November
    2014 ("The debate about which generation is more
    suited to military service does not originate from
    an actual gap between age groups. It stems from a
    timeless attitude problem of those who loudly and
    without listening invade the space of those trying
    to get work done.").

2   Sexual Assault Response Coordinator (SARC).
    A position created to deal with a problem that
    was only extant in the minds of the likes of
    Barbara Boxer. The UCMJ was already capable of
    successfully prosecuting rapists – hell, I personally
    prosecuted and defended dozens of cases in
    Germany in the mid-90 – but, in my opinion,
    morning-after regrets by a female does not make

her a victim. This is especially true when her male partner was just as drunk as she was the night before.

CHAPTER SEVENTEEN

1 Delingpole, James, "US Attorney General: We've 'Discussed' Prosecuting Climate Change Deniers", *Breitbart*, March 10, 2016.

CHAPTER TWENTY-TWO

1 *Graham v. Connor*, 490 US 386, the seminal United States Supreme Court case on use of force.
2 Chapter Twenty-Six Chapter
3 Tzu, Sun. *The Art of War*. Translated by Samuel B. Griffith. London: Oxford University Press, 1963.
4 Schwabe, Alexander, "The Cowboy and the Shepherd," Spiegel Online International, April 16, 2008.
5 http://en.wikiquote.org/wiki/Winston_Churchill, unsourced.
6 McShane, Thomas W., "International Law and the New World Order: Redefining Sovereignty,", reprinted in US Army War College Guide to National Security Issues, Vol. 2: *National Security Policy and Strategy*, Edited by J. Boone Bartholomees Jr, Carlisle barracks, PA (June 2008).
7 Churchill, Winston, *The Grand Alliance*, Edited by John Keegan, Houghton Mifflin Books, New York, 1986
8 http://www.icc-cpi.int/chambers/judges.html According to article 38 of the Rome Statute, the

18 judges of the Court elected the Presidency the 11 March 2006. It is composed of Judge Philippe Kirsch (Canada) as President; Judge Akua Kuenyehia (Ghana) as First Vice-President; and Judge René Blattmann (Bolivia) as Second Vice-President.

9 http://en.wikiquote.org/wiki/Winston_ Churchill#The_World_War_II_years, Speech broadcast on October 1, 1939.

10 http://www.oracle.com/industries/government/ Oracle_in_Homeland_Security.pdf, Leveraging Information Technology to Secure America (2003), quoting Sir Winston Churchill.

11 Such as "nation building" of the unwilling or ungovernable (Afghanistan circa 2008) or the internal squabbles of sovereign states (Serbia 1999).

12 Cicero, Marcus Tullius Cicero, *Defense Speeches*, Translated by D. H. Berry,

13 London: Oxford University Press, 2000 Markus Tullius Cicero, Cicero: On Behalf of Milo, 60 BCE.

14 Justinian: Digest of Roman Law, 529 CE.

15 Ex. 22:2-3.

16 Cantrell, Charles L., The Right to Bear Arms: A Reply, 53 Wis. B. Bull. 21-26 (Oct. 1980);

17 See also, 3 Blackstone, William, *Commentaries on the Laws of England*, at 141 (1766).

18 *Id.*

19 Foster, Sir Michael, Crown Cases, 273-274 (London 1776).

20 Locke, John, *Two Treatises of Government*, "The State of War," §16 (1689).

21 St. Thomas Aquinas, *Summa Theologica II-II*, Q. 64, art. 7 (13th century).

22 Thomas Jefferson, in a letter to William Johnson, June 12, 1823.

23 1 Hawkins, Pleas of the Crown, Ch. 28, §14 (7th ed. 1795).

24 3 Blackstone, William, Commentaries on the Laws of England, at 141 (1766).

25 Samuel Adams, The Rights of Colonists, November 20, 1772.

26 Letter from Daniel Webster, Secretary of State, to Henry Fox, British Minister in Washington, April 24, 1841, reprinted in 2 John Bassett Moore, A Digest of International Law 409, 412 (1906).

27 *See* International Military Tribunal (Nuremberg), Judgment and Sentences, reprinted in 41 Am J Intl L 172, 205 (1947) ("Preventive action in foreign territory is justified only in case of 'an instant and overwhelming necessity for self-defense, leaving no choice of means, and no moment for deliberation.'"), quoting John Bassett Moore, 2 International Law Digest § 217 at 412 (GPO 1906).

28 Brunson MacChesney, "Some Comments on the 'Quarantine' of Cuba, *American Journal of International Law*, 57 (No. 3 1963), 593.

29 Gravelle, James Francis, The Falkland (Malvinas) Islands: An International Law Analysis of the Dispute Between Argentina and Great Britain." *Military Law Review*, 107 (1985), 57.

30 UN Charter, Article 2(4).

31 Clemmons, Byard Q. & Brown, Gary, "Rethinking International Self Defense: The UN's Emerging Role," NAV. L. REV. 217, 218 (1998). "Self defense is so much a part of state sovereignty that it would be recognized even absent Article 51."

32 George W. Bush, The National Security Strategy of the United States of America (Washington: The White House, March 2006), 18.

33 *Bowers v. DeVito*, 686 F.2d 616 (7th Cir. 1982).

34 *District of Columbia v. Heller*, 554 US 570 (2008).

CHAPTER TWENTY-NINE

1 ESPN fired Kurt Schilling for simply stating well-grounded scientific and moral truths on a social media site, "A man is a man no matter what they call themselves. I don't care what they are, who they sleep with, men's room was designed for the penis, women's not so much. Now you need laws telling us differently? Pathetic." Nothing that leftist politicized "sports" network does surprises us anymore.

CHAPTER THIRTY-ONE

1 Page, Susan, "Air Force secretary supports lifting transgender ban", *USA Today*, December 10, 2014.

2 As quoted in *An American Knight: The Life of Colonel John W. Ripley, USMC, by* Norman J. Fulkerson (The American Society for the Defense of Tradition, Family and Property).

CHAPTER THIRTY-FIVE

1   In October 2011, Havard spoke to the entire resident Army War College Class of 2012. His lecture was one of the highest-rated events of that year and can be accessed at http://www.youtube.com/watch?v=72VBdMoDfbY.

2   William Penn, quoted from Thomas Clarkson, *Memoirs of the Private and Public Life of William Penn* (London: Richard Taylor and Co., 1813) Vol. I, p. 303.

3   William Stearns Davis, *Readings in Ancient History: Illustrative Extracts from the Sources, Vol. 2: Greece and the East* (Boston: Allyn and Bacon, 1912), pp. 58--61.

4   Such as Mikey Weinstein of the misleadingly named "Military Religious Freedom Foundation."

THE CARDINAL VIRTUES

1   Fraser, George MacDonald, *Quartered Safe Out Here: A Harrowing Tale of World War II*, Skyhorse Publishing, 2007.

2   2 Peter 3:5.

3   St. Mark the Hermit, *De lege spirituali*, 172.

4   If one places a bullfrog into a pan of boiling water, the frog will jump out. If, however, one puts the frog into a pot of cool water, then gradually turns up the temperature, the frog will peacefully stay in the pot until cooked to death. It is the allegory that points out the dangers of incrementalism.

5   Isaiah 5:20, Douay-Rheims Bible translation.

6 Words have meaning, so the military's continual misuse of the word "gender" (which means masculine or feminine) in place of "sex" (which designates whether someone is male or female) is both misleading and a further sign of incompetence. If the military really wants "gender" equality, then we will end up with an emasculated force where overtly manly or womanly traits will not be tolerated. Perhaps, this is exactly what some of those advocating transformation mean.

7 See Grady, John, "Navy and Marine Officials Discuss Integrating Women Into More Roles," *Proceedings,* October 2014. "The Marine Corps is using a social science approach to introduce women into expanded roles in the service, a plans officer in the Corps' force innovation office told a conference of military reporters and editors Friday in Washington, D.C. "[Because] we are very interested in morale," Lt. Col. Michael Samarov said, the idea is to prove to other members of a squad that "the new member can do the job as well or better than the others. I think that will settle the issue" of placing women in positions and with units that had been previously closed to them."

8 Petronio, Katie, "Get Over It! We Are Not All Created Equal," *Marine Corps Gazette,* January 2013.

EPILOGUE

1 Arnn, Larry P., *Churchill's Trial: Winston Churchill and the Salvation of Free Government,* Nelson Books, Nashville (2015), p. 66.

2 Matthew 16:18 "And I say to thee: That thou art Peter; and upon this rock I will build my church, and the gates of hell shall not prevail against it."

3 Lieutenant Colonel John Taylor, USA (Ret.) significantly contributed to certain chapters in this book.

4 I tried to duly note those in which he did, but feel certain he influenced many more. John is a fellow paratrooper and peace officer. He has served in many great units, to include 1st Special Forces Operational Detachment – Delta (Delta Force). 3rd Special Forces Group (Airborne), and the 82nd Airborne Division. He was also an integral part of Task Force Bowie, one of the lead Special Operations Forces units into Afghanistan in 2001. He is a true friend and warrior.

WORLD AHEAD *press*

Self-publishing means that you have the freedom to blaze your own trail as an author. But that doesn't mean you should go it alone. By choosing to publish with WORLD AHEAD PRESS, you partner with WND—one of the most powerful and influential brands on the Internet.

If you liked this book and want to publish your own, WORLD AHEAD PRESS, co-publishing division of WND Books, is right for you. WORLD AHEAD PRESS will turn your manuscript into a high-quality book and then promote it through its broad reach into conservative and Christian markets worldwide.

IMAGINE YOUR BOOK ALONGSIDE THESE AUTHORS!

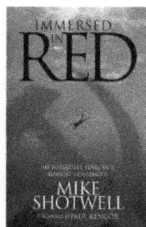

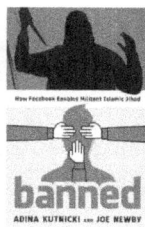

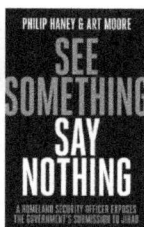

www.ingramcontent.com/pod-product-compliance
Lightning Source LLC
Chambersburg PA
CBHW031158270326
41931CB00006B/323